MW00896424

13 Most Haunted

HOTELS & INNS OF NEW ENGLAND

13 Most Haunted

HOTELS & INNS OF NEW ENGLAND

To Jackie!
Happy Hauntings

Sam Baltrusis

Sam Baltrusis

ACKNOWLEDGEMENTS

Writing *13 Most Haunted Hotels & Inns of New England* felt like an epic two-year journey of self discovery. It started with a sobbing ghost girl at the Pilgrim House Inn in Newport, Rhode Island in 2015 and ended with a balding, old-man spirit approaching me at The Kennebunk Inn in Maine. I worked as a part-time night auditor at two allegedly haunted hotels, Hotel 140 and the Constitution Inn, and I want to thank the staff and visitors for the graveyard-shift inspiration. Special thanks to Joni Mayhan, author of *Bones in the Basement*, for penning the book's foreword and creating an honorable mention list of haunted hotels in a chapter called *The Others*. Mayhan's wisdom and hands-on experience at several of New England's most haunted locations is featured throughout the manuscript. Photographers Frank C. Grace and Jason Baker deserve a supernatural slap on the back for capturing the eerie aesthetic of the main haunts in the *13 Most Haunted* countdown. Carol Matsumoto and her husband Ted, innkeepers at Connecticut's Captain Grant's Inn, were amazing hosts. Ed Maas, the owner of the family-run Orleans Waterfront Inn, also deserves major props for opening his extremely haunted doors to my spirit squad, which included Mike Cultrera, former technical director of my weekly radio show and travel partner. Patricia and John Basiliere from the Black Swan in New Hampshire were also great resources. Major thanks to the handful of paranormal investigators and researchers who helped make *13 Most Haunted Hotels & Inns of New England* a reality, including Jack Kenna and Ellen MacNeil from S.P.I.R.I.T.S. of New England, Sue Vickery and psychic-medium Lucky Belcamino from the Lizzie Borden B&B, *New England Folklore*'s Peter Muise, James Annitto, Russ Stiver, Kristene Gulla, Colleen Costello, Michael Baker from Para-Boston, investigator Rachel Hoffman from Paranormal Xpeditions 2.0, Ron Kolek from *Ghost Chronicles*, Amy Bruni and Adam Berry from TLC's *Kindred Spirits* and Scott Porter and Tim Weisberg from Destination America's *Haunted Towns*. The team from the syndicated TV show *What's New? Massachusetts* and Somerville Media Center (SMC), including my co-host Sharon Fillyaw, deserve an old-school high five for helping me with the TV show component of the project. Thanks to my mother, Deborah Hughes Dutcher, for being there when I need her most and my friends for their continued support. My friends at Wicked Good Books in Salem also deserve kudos for carrying my books and hosting the Wicked Salem Tour. Special thanks to Andrew Warburton, editor of my first six books and long-time friend. He and I had an extremely spirited stay at the Pilgrim House Inn in Newport, and, in many ways, that visit was the inspiration for the book. Of course, I continue to thank the legendary author Stephen King for traumatizing me as a kid with the horror classic, *The Shining*. For *13 Most Haunted Hotels & Inns of New England*, I would like to add King's short story, "1408," or what he calls the "Ghostly Room at the Inn," to my list of inspiration. I hope you enjoy your stay.

TABLE OF CONTENTS

FOREWORD

"As someone who has experienced both the best and the worst the paranormal world has to offer, I encourage you to be careful in your journeys. The world of the dead surrounds us, and it isn't always a warm, welcoming place ... especially in haunted hotels."

—Joni Mayhan, author of "Ghost Magnet" and "Bones in the Basement"

Road-weary travelers are often uneasy when they check into their hotel room for the night.

Something doesn't seem right. They feel as though they're being watched. Lights turn on and off without anyone touching them, and their possessions are moved in the middle of the night. If the travelers sleep at all, their dreams are filled with horrendous nightmares. When they wake up the next morning, they feel tired and drained.

Room with a boo? Intense emotions ranging from an argument to a suicide can leave a psychic imprint at haunted hotels like the Providence Biltmore in Rhode Island. *Photo by Jason Baker.*

Does this sound familiar to you? If so, you've probably spent the night in a haunted hotel.

Haunted hotels are far more prevalent than most people would imagine. If you consider the sheer number of people who stay in them, it makes perfect sense. A normal house might encounter forty or fifty guests during the history of its existence, while a hotel will shelter that number in several days. Over a period of years, hundreds of thousands of guests with varying degrees of mental and physical health have passed through those doors, substantially increasing the odds of a haunting.

While the majority of the hauntings can be attributed to former owners or guests who spent a great deal of time at the location, many others come from a surprising source. I believe that some of them are suicide victims.

Someone who premeditated their suicide might choose to perform the deed away from their family and friends. They might check into a hotel, thinking it would be better for the housekeeper to find them instead of their family. However, once completed, they freeze in front of the white light, choosing to stay earthbound instead. They might remember their teachings from church, telling them that suicide is a mortal sin. If they cross through the white light, will they find themselves in heaven or hell?

When it comes to paranormal activity, the type of hotel doesn't seem to matter. I've stayed at nice hotels and the kind you wouldn't want your dog to stay in. They're all equally haunted. All it takes is one ghost to make a sensitive's night a living hell.

As someone who can feel spiritual energy, I'm a magnet for the dead. They hone in on me in droves, hoping for a plethora of things. Some want to simply make contact or pass along a message to a living loved one. Others have a darker intent.

I used to enjoy spending the night in haunted locations. It gave me full access to the resident ghosts. As my abilities began to develop, this changed quickly.

The minute I close my eyes, I can feel them come closer. They drift from the dark corners of the room, separating themselves from the shadows as they approach my bed. If I'm lucky, I can push them away, but that isn't always the case. Many times, they will latch onto me like parasites and pull as much energy from me as possible; leaving me drained the next day.

People who investigate the paranormal call this phenomenon a paranormal hangover. You feel depleted of energy, especially after investigating an especially active location. In this case, the ghosts have learned how to utilize their energy sources so they can perform more ghostly deeds.

Since I've learned the valuable lessons in how to properly ground and shield myself, some of this has lessened, but not completely. Are the ghosts using my energy to do the things I'm asking them to do? Does every EVP come at a cost?

Part of my fascination with the paranormal field revolves around the "why" factor. I'm interested in learning more, which will hopefully help me and others better explain the experiences we continue to have as we investigate haunted locations.

If you do plan to visit one of the locations in Sam's book, take as many precautions as possible.

Here are some tips:

- Learn how to ground and shield yourself. Imagine a white light above you and absorb it into the crown of your head with every breath you take. As you pull the white light inside you, push all excess energy that doesn't serve you out through the soles of your feet. Once you've finished, surround yourself with a bubble of protective white light.
- Carry religious medallions or protective stones that make you feel safe.
- Pray and/or ask your spirit guides to help you stay protected.
- Never offer your energy to the resident ghosts. This is like handing over your bank card to a stranger and telling them to just take what they need. You will be sorry if you do this because they will often drain you dry.
- Don't provoke the ghosts. Even though you might have watched this method used successfully on paranormal television shows, it seldom results in anything good. Without fully knowing who you are antagonizing, you could be poking an angry bear or a sad lost soul who only wants to be left alone.
- Get enough rest the night before, and eat healthy foods the day of the event. Keeping your body strong is key to keeping your spiritual boundaries high. Also, avoid investigating when you are feeling depressed, tired or out-of-sorts. When you feel this way, your energy level is already low, and it will be easier for them to attach to you.
- Despite your protection methods, it's common to feel drained the day after an investigation or an overnight stay at a haunted hotel. Your recovery is as important as your precautionary methods.
- Get enough rest afterward. If you stay out until four in the morning and don't get into bed until six, it stands to reason that you will need to sleep until one or two in the afternoon. Many people can't do this because it interferes with their internal body clocks. The best thing to do is sleep as long as you can, and then get up and make the best of it.
- Keeping yourself fully hydrated will help as well. Even though you might crave coffee or energy drinks, stick with water until you're fully hydrated. Caffeine can act as a diuretic, causing you to dehydrate even further. Drink plenty of water.
- Get out and stay busy. When faced with a paranormal hangover, most people just want to vegetate on the sofa in front of the television all day. While it does help to kill the time, it won't help you recover. Get out and enjoy the sunshine and fresh air. You'll be amazed at how much better you feel.

- Eat a balanced diet that is high in protein. Our bodies crave protein when our energy is depleted. Proteins such as lean meats, nuts and eggs can provide you with a boost to help you recover your energy.
- Stay away from refined sugars and processed, salty foods. I always crave soda and chips when I'm feeling energy depleted, but neither serves to help me regain my energy. Wholesome foods, like green leafy vegetables, fruits high in Vitamin C and plenty of water are your best allies for regaining your energy.
- I also find that an investigation often disrupts my normal sleep pattern, leaving me off schedule for days later. I combat this by taking a melatonin supplement before bedtime on a daily basis.
- Go to bed at your usual time the night after an investigation. Fight the urge to nap during the day. This will only prevent you from getting to sleep later when it's your normal bedtime. Avoid watching television, using a computer or drinking caffeinated drinks several hours prior to bedtime.
- If you feel as though something has followed you home, waste no time. Find a good psychic medium to help you separate yourself from the energy.

As someone who has experienced both the best and the worst the paranormal world has to offer, I encourage you to be careful in your journeys. The world of the dead surrounds us, and it isn't always a warm, welcoming place … especially in haunted hotels.

Joni Mayhan is a paranormal investigator and the best-selling author of sixteen paranormal books. To learn more about her and her books, check out her website *JoniMayhan.com*.

Author Sam Baltrusis received a mysterious package in the mail from an anonymous source in the United Kingdom. It was a key to one of New England's most haunted hotels. *Photo by Jason Baker.*

INTRODUCTION

"Some of my paranormal friends are 'ghost magnets.' I don't necessarily attract or repel things that go bump in the night. My gift is that I intuitively know where the spirits are, and I inexplicably find myself in those places."

—Sam Baltrusis, author of "13 Most Haunted Hotels & Inns of New England"

Want to see if a "room with a boo" is truly haunted? Work the graveyard shift at an allegedly haunted hotel.

For a few months in 2017, I signed on as a night auditor at two boo-tique inns, including the Hotel 140 in the Back Bay. Right above the front desk is the Lyric Stage Company theater. Multiple times in the wee hours of the night, I encountered a female spirit who'd mysteriously try to lead me upstairs. I'm not sure what her deal was, but she was desperately trying to communicate with me.

One Monday night in May 2017 when I was working the overnight shift at Hotel 140, I met Lyric Stage Company of Boston's associate production manager, Stephanie Hettrick. We started chatting, and within the first few minutes, she revealed to me that my hunch was true: the former YWCA turned hotel is in fact haunted. "We call her Alice," Hettrick said, speaking quietly so her friend couldn't hear her talking about the building's resident ghost. "She doesn't like me, but she likes my boss. He was away for a week and caused all sorts of problems. Things would mysteriously move. Lights would turn on and off. We blamed it on Alice."

When I asked her if she knew anything about Alice's backstory, Hettrick said she strongly believed the female spirit was in her early to late twenties. I asked her how she knew so many details about the resident spirit, and the production manager smiled. "Because I've seen her," she said, pointing to the second-floor mezzanine level of the hotel and the side-stairs area Alice is known to frequent. "She's wearing white, and sometimes when I'm here late at night in the theater, I will see her out of the corner of my eye."

Hettrick's friend, who was in the ladies' room behind Hotel 140's front desk, ran out in a tizzy. "Are you talking about ghosts? If you are then I'm going to leave now." Her friend was joking, but you could see she was obviously creeped out by the hotel's resident spirit.

Of course, Hotel 140 isn't the only overnight haunt in the Boston area that's reported to have supernatural activity. Several of the Hub's haunted dormitories, including Boston University's Kilachand Hall (formerly Shelton Hall and my sophomore-year college dorm) and Berklee College of Music's 150 Massachusetts Ave., had former lives as hotels. The Charlesgate, Emerson College's "devilish dormitory," which has been converted into upscale condominiums, was built in 1891 as a fin de siècle hotel and boasted upscale accommodations for Boston's elite and then deteriorated during the Depression before housing college students.

Scene from the movie *1408*? Author Sam Baltrusis unlocks the secrets hidden in New England's blood-stained hotels including the Providence Biltmore. *Photo by Jason Baker.*

When it comes to haunted dorms, school spirits reflect school spirit. Based on my experience as a paranormal researcher and as the author of eight historical-based ghost books, I've unwittingly become a voice for New England's spirit squad. *We got spirits, yes we do.*

While writing *13 Most Haunted Hotels & Inns of New England*, I've been featured on two national paranormal TV shows, including Destination America's *Haunted Towns*, which focused on Salem. I also made a cameo on the Travel Channel recounting my face-to-face encounter with a lady in white in the Witch City's Old Burying Point on Charter Street. In 2012, I was featured as Boston's paranormal expert on the Biography Channel's *Haunted Encounters.*

How can one person have so many experiences of New England's ghosts? I'm mysteriously called to these haunted locations. It's both a blessing and a curse.

Some of my paranormal friends are "ghost magnets." I don't necessarily attract or repel things that go bump in the night. My gift is that I intuitively know where the spirits are, and I inexplicably find myself in those places. Usually I end up in locations that aren't necessarily known to be haunted but turn out to be extremely active from a paranormal perspective.

I guess I have built-in "ghostdar."

In addition to my part-time gig at Hotel 140, my built-in ghost GPS led me to a hotel that's close to one of my favorite local haunts, the USS *Constitution* in the Boston Navy Yard. A stone's throw from the extremely active "Old Ironsides," the Constitution Inn had an under-the-radar paranormal reputation of sorts thanks to its close proximity to U.S. Navy's crown jewel, Charlestown's iconic wooden-hulled, three-masted heavy frigate.

When I first applied to be the hotel's part-time night auditor, my future boss nodded when I asked if the Constitution Inn had any resident ghosts. "Talk to the ladies in housekeeping," my manager said with a sheepish smile. "They swear they've seen something downstairs."

After several overnights working at the Constitution Inn, I invited several friends to investigate with me at the hotel, which included a visit to the supposedly haunted laundry room. It was a spirited night to say the least.

One of the guests, Cynthia Olson Mattison, had a weird communication during the investigation led by the S.P.I.R.I.T.S. of New England team at the Constitution Inn. Someone or something typed "hi" on her phone when she left it on the table. It was very strange and the beginning of communications with two possible spirits at the inn.

"We know for a fact there are other buildings within the Navy Yard that have activity," explained Jack Kenna, investigator with S.P.I.R.I.T.S. of New England. "Back in July of 2010 when we investigated the *Constitution*, some of the ship's officers told us about several other locations in the shipyard they had experiences in and believed were haunted," Kenna continued. "There's a lot of history in Charlestown and, of course, the entire Boston area. Some of that history goes all the way back to the 1600s. I do believe that this part of Boston could very well hold some of the most interesting and intense paranormal activity in the Boston area."

Kenna and Ellen MacNeil gave a spine-tingling lecture about their investigation on board the USS *Constitution*. During their discussion at the Constitution Inn, the door leading into the conference room mysteriously swung open and then closed.

Was it a spirit? Perhaps,. I do know that somewhere deep in our subconscious, ghost stories satiate a primitive desire to know that life exists after death. Based on my experience working overnights at two potentially haunted hotels, I do believe that inns have a proclivity for hauntings based purely on the numbers of people who pass through them. Extreme emotions leave a psychic imprint. An intense moment—like a murder, suicide or even a wedding—could leave an indelible mark.

However, the residual haunting theory apparently doesn't apply to all of New England's historic overnight haunts. If I had to choose one hotel in New England that I thought would be haunted but isn't, it would be Boston's Liberty Hotel. Based purely on its history, the Hub's "most wanted" should also be Boston's most haunted. But it's not.

Located at 215 Charles St., Boston's posh Liberty Hotel had a past life as the Charles Street Jail. But is it haunted? *Photo courtesy of the Boston Public Library, Print Department.*

The Liberty Hotel—formerly the Charles Street Jail, which housed a rogues' gallery of former clientele, including several mob bosses; a German U-boat captain who killed himself with shards from his sunglasses soon after being captured in 1945; Frank Abagnale Jr., the notorious con artist played by Leonardo DiCaprio in the flick *Catch Me If You Can*; and Boston mayor James Michael Curley, who served time for fraud in 1904—was reborn as a luxury hotel in 2007.

However, have the ghosts from the jail's dodgy past left the massive gray granite and brick structure since closing its doors in 1990?

Some guests aren't convinced. "When I told my husband about this place, he looked at me like I was nuts. I don't know if we'll ever actually stay at The Liberty, as it has to be haunted, and I'm a big chicken," wrote Paloma Contrera from *High Gloss Magazine*. "One hundred fifty plus years of poor living conditions for angry criminals… That is a sure-fire recipe for mean ghosts."

When the jail opened in 1851, it was praised as a world-class model of prison architecture. Built in the shape of a cross, the Charles Street Jail had a ninety-foot-high central rotunda and four wings of cells. In the late 1880s, each of the 220 rooms housed one inmate. However, things changed as the jail aged and fell into disrepair. In the 1970s, a riot broke out, and inmates sued over the building's squalid, overcrowded conditions. A federal judge ordered the structure closed in 1973, but it took seventeen years for many of the prisoners to find new homes. After a five-year, $150 million renovation, the former lockup reopened as the Liberty Hotel, which tipped its hat to the building's captivating but dark past with a restaurant called Clink and a bar named Alibi. However, only eighteen of the hotel's 298 rooms are housed in the building's original jail.

In an attempt to rid the building of any negative residual energy haunting the hotel, management brought in a team of Buddhist monks to perform a cleansing ritual. "Clearly, there are some very dark and depressing elements to this building, and we have to be careful how we tell its story," said Stuart Meyerson, former general manager, in the British newspaper *The Independent*. "I don't think everyone enjoyed staying here."

Former Liberty Hotel patron Charlene Swauger of Albuquerque believed the cleansing ritual worked. "I didn't discover any ghosts or anything," she told the *Associated Press*. "I thought it was very clever."

As far as lingering spirits are concerned, the Liberty's former marketing manager insisted that no shadow figures can be seen walking the iron-railing balconies, which were once catwalks where guards stood watch over the inmates. "Believe it or not, there have been no unusual occurrences here at the hotel," she told me.

However, tour buses passing by the 150-year-old structure allude to the Liberty's spirited past, including a mention that the hotel's courtyard was formerly a gallows, and travel journalists play with the Charles Street Jail's creepy vibe. "The Liberty Hotel, Boston's reconfigured former jail, once housed characters like the Boston Strangler," mused the *Austin American-Statesman* in an article called "Boston's Scariest Haunts" in October 2010. "Guests say they gather in the lobby champagne bar just because there's always safety in numbers."

Yes, the Liberty Hotel has a macabre past. It should be haunted, but it's not.

The Borden Flats Light is a historic and potentially haunted lighthouse on the Taunton River in Fall River, Massachusetts. *Photo by Frank C. Grace.*

A handful of potential locations in New England didn't make the *13 Most Haunted* list because they're technically not inns or hotels ... they're lighthouses. At least two haunts available for overnight stays—Rose Island Lighthouse in Newport, Rhode Island and Borden Flats Light in Fall River, Massachusetts— reportedly have lingering spirits.

Built in 1870, the Rose Island Lighthouse in Newport's Narragansett Bay is said to be home to former keeper Charles Curtis who still opens and closes doors even though his last day on the job was in 1918. Visitors who take a ferry to Rose Island can even spend the night in the allegedly haunted barracks formerly used to quarantine dysentery victims. Over at Borden Flats Light in Fall River, paranormal investigators have reported what sounded like a man whistling and a little girl laughing. Sensitives claim that Captain John Paul, keeper of the Borden Flats Light between 1912–1927, continues to keep watch in the afterlife.

Haunted lighthouses? Yes, it's a no-brainer.

Jeremy D'Entremont, author and historian of the American Lighthouse Foundation, jokingly told me that people can find at least one ghost story associated with each of the dozens of lighthouses scattered throughout New England if they dig deep enough.

"Just imagine living at an isolated, offshore lighthouse all year round, through storms and all kinds of extreme conditions," he told me. "Such an existence could easily cause the imagination to play tricks. But I do believe that many of these stories are at least partially true. Some people think that the ocean is a good conductor of paranormal energy. I'm not sure about that, but lighthouses are among the oldest structures in many of our coastal communities, and their human history is dramatic and full of emotion."

The historian told me that he's heard several strange-but-true tales from the various structures. "Many of these stories seem to point to a lighthouse keeper of the past who continues to 'keep watch,' even after his death," he said.

D'Entremont, the go-to expert for New England lighthouses, said he even had a close encounter himself while giving a tour at his home haunt for fifteen years, Portsmouth Harbor Light in New Castle, New Hampshire. "One day I was giving a tour for a married couple in the middle of the afternoon. We were at the top of the stairs, in the watch room. I was leaning against a ladder and telling them some of the history of the place," he recalled. "As I was talking, a low, gravelly, male voice from my right said, 'Hello.' I stopped and asked the couple if they'd heard anything."

The husband in the group swore he also heard a man say "hello," whereas his wife didn't hear a peep. "We looked down the stairs and outside, and there was nobody else anywhere near the lighthouse. A few other people have had similar experiences," he added.

Of course, D'Entremont said extreme isolation could factor into each alleged ghost sighting. "I definitely think living at a remote, isolated location can play tricks on your imagination," he continued. "I have no doubt that some ghost stories were based on strange but natural sights and sounds experienced by the keepers and their families. I also think that keepers and family members shared stories, and they are prone to exaggeration as they're passed down."

As far as my personal experiences writing *13 Most Haunted Hotels and Inns of New England* are concerned, my abilities as an empath gradually heightened over the two-year period I spent visiting these extremely haunted hotels. When I first started, I felt like John Cusack's character Mike Enslin in the movie *1408*. I was still somewhat of a skeptic. However, I had several life-changing experiences with the paranormal along the way.

When I visited Fall River's iconic murder house, the Lizzie Borden B&B, I was expecting to be underwhelmed. I wasn't. In fact, within the first few minutes, I spotted a shadow figure dart past, and I connected deeply with Lizzie Borden's stepmother, Abby, in the John Morse room. I was in tears when I walked over to the scene of the crime.

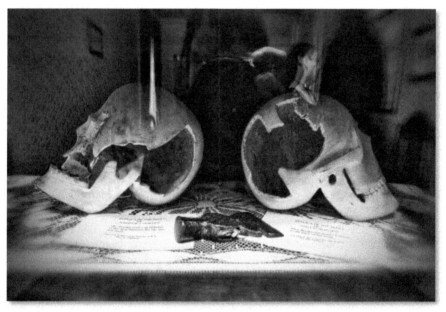

Sue Vickery, a tour guide at the Lizzie Borden B&B in Fall River, has been featured on several television shows, including TLC's *Kindred Spirits* where she recounted her face-to-face encounters with ghosts at New England's notorious murder house. *Photo by Frank C. Grace.*

Sue Vickery, a tour guide at the Lizzie Borden B&B, said my sensitivities were spot on. "Yes, it's a very common experience," she told me. "I've also been overcome with sadness on occasion in that room. I've had guests walk through that doorway and break out in tears."

Vickery, who was recently featured on TLC's *Kindred Spirits* with Amy Bruni and Adam Berry, said the hauntings at the Lizzie Borden B&B live up to the building's national reputation. "The Bordens are very much still a presence here," she said. "I've spoken with Andrew, Abby, Lizzie and occasionally Emma through the spirit box. I've witnessed black mist and white mist. I've had voices speak when no one is in the house. Footsteps are common. Doors open and close. I've been touched on numerous occasions as well."

In addition to my visit to the Lizzie Borden B&B, my most profound personal experience occurred during an overnight stay at Captain Grant's Inn in Preston, Connecticut. I somehow channeled the spirit of the inn's resident gay ghost, Liam. I first connected with him during an impromptu interview with the innkeeper, Carol Matsumoto, in the kitchen. During our chat, it felt as if someone hugged me from behind. Matsumoto jokingly said, "oh, that's just Liam," and I mused that Liam needed to learn a thing or two about boundaries.

I immediately felt connected with him as he led me to an open field behind the historic structure. During my trek out to the cemetery hidden behind the inn, I touched a tree, and it felt as if I was being transported back in time. Based on my vision, Liam loved to fish, and he was attacked by the locals for being different. He desperately wanted to tell me his story. I was standing in the middle of the field, shivering in the beauty and the madness of the moment.

After connecting with Liam, I headed inside and immediately passed out. It was a deep sleep in which I experienced full-blown spirit communication with the inn's resident ghosts. In the dream, I was hanging out with Liam, and he was wearing an outfit that appeared to be from the eighteenth century.

The following morning during breakfast, Carol asked me if I was out fishing in the brook behind the cemetery. I was shocked. Fishing? "Yes, we thought we saw you out there with a fishing pole." I'm not into fishing, but Liam definitely was. I held my breath.

Chapter 1

LIZZIE BORDEN B&B
FALL RIVER, MASSACHUSETTS
MOST HAUNTED: #1

"Maggie, come quick! Father's dead. Somebody came in and killed him."

—Lizzie Borden's words to Bridget Sullivan on August 4, 1892

I didn't want to do it. The idea of spending the night at a location that I believed was one of the most haunted in New England was enough to send shivers down my spine. In fact, I chickened out of two previously planned overnight stays at the Lizzie Borden B&B while writing *13 Most Haunted Hotels & Inns of New England*.

Then I started having the dreams … again. I've had them in the past, but the latest involved an unlikely player in the horrific double murder that rocked Fall River. The Bordens' maid, Bridget Sullivan, was reaching out to me when I was asleep. Her specter was pinning me to the bed, showing me what had unfolded that infamous morning in August 1892.

According to Sullivan's court testimony, she was taking a nap in her third-floor room after allegedly cleaning windows when Lizzie's stepmother, Abby, was savagely murdered in the second-floor guest room. Sullivan, nicknamed "Maggie" by the Borden girls, ascended a separate stairwell, avoiding the crime scene in the present-day John Morse room.

At 11:10 a.m. on August 4, 1892, Bridget heard Lizzie call from downstairs, "Maggie, come quick! Father's dead. Somebody came in and killed him."

In my dream, Sullivan kept pointing to the closet in her bedroom. She was trying to show me that there was a well or cistern in there, and, for some mysterious reason, the closet was significant.

My overnight stay at the Lizzie Borden B&B was quite an emotional tour de force. Within the first few minutes of walking into the house, I saw a shadow figure dart past the murder couch and heard a female voice say my name. For the record, the spirit had a very thick New England accent. My friend Lucky Belcamino, the official psychic of the haunted hotspot, was giving readings at the inn during my mid-July visit, and she filled me in on the hauntings.

The Lizzie Borden murder house, now a bed and breakfast, is located at 92 Second St. in Fall River. *Photo by Frank C. Grace.*

Based on seven years of firsthand personal experience, the psychic-medium told me that the activity in the house is amplified in the weeks leading up to the anniversary of the double murders.

"I do believe that during the summer months, when there are a lot of people booking rooms and attending the tours, the spirits are curious and love the energy in the home," Belcamino said. "They will be more apt to communicate with those that are respectful and want to know the truth."

Within the first hour, I visited the John Morse crime-scene room, and I was literally brought to tears by the spirit of Abby Borden. Based on her portrayal in pop culture, I always thought she was a wicked-stepmother archetype. I was wrong. Her energy was sweet, and the sadness I felt was somehow related to how Lizzie and her sister Emma hadn't accepted her as a mother figure.

Based on my overnight stay, I can safely say that the Lizzie Borden B&B has somehow become extremely haunted. Why?

Ron Kolek, author of *Ghost Chronicles* and longtime paranormal investigator, told me a theory a few years ago as to why certain locations seem to become progressively more paranormally active once they appear on TV. Are investigators—like the team from the Travel Channel's *Ghost Adventures*—somehow stirring up activity in locations that hadn't previously had histories of paranormal shenanigans?

"Look at the Houghton Mansion," Kolek responded. "I investigated that place years ago before it became a regular location for paranormal groups. I've gone back there recently, and it's completely different now. There's stuff there now that wasn't there before. I think these paranormal teams are bringing something with them," he said, alluding to para-celeb investigators who somehow conjure negative energy at Houghton Mansion that didn't exist years ago. "Are they bringing stowaway entities with them? I think so," Kolek continued. "It's like negative spirits know where to go to get more attention."

My first thought after chatting with Kolek was about the Lizzie Borden house. It's one of those locations with reported paranormal activity that has become progressively more active, even sinister, over the years.

Although she was tried and acquitted of the gruesome murder at her 1845-era Victorian home on Second Street in Fall River, the hatchet-wielding Lizzie Borden never shook her "forty whacks" claim to fame that she hacked up her father and stepmother on August 4, 1892. In addition to her chop-chop notoriety, Borden has been rumored to have had an intimate relationship with actress Nance O'Neil. However, this scandalous affair is unsubstantiated.

"We don't have any real evidence regarding Lizzie's orientation," said Bill Pavao, historian and former curator at the Lizzie Borden House. Pavao actually lived in the home for several years before it became a recurring location on all of the television investigation shows. He told me that he'd never experienced anything paranormal during his long-term stay.

However, psychic-medium Lucky Belcamino said the vibe in the home has changed in recent years.

"I connect on a more personal level with Lizzie and the uncle, John Morse," she said. "I will sit in their rooms and do spirit-box sessions and talk to them like I'm talking to friends."

When the psychic-medium asked Lizzie what she was doing during the murder-suicide, Borden's spirit told Belcamino that "she was eating six pears," Lucky said. "She's playful at times and sometimes a little rude and abrasive. Sometimes she will not say anything."

As far as ghosts are concerned, visitors claim to have heard sounds of a woman weeping and have spotted a full-bodied apparition wearing Victorian-era clothing dusting the furniture. Phantom footsteps storming down the stairs and doors mysteriously opening and closing have also been reported. Also, guests have heard muffled conversations coming from vacant rooms. Perhaps it's the spirits of Borden and Sullivan making a post-mortem pact to hide the bloody hatchet.

Or, maybe it's something more sinister?

In my opinion, the basement is the most active location in the house. In fact, when I first opened the door after midnight, I heard a loud hissing, and my group of amateur investigators captured an EVP, or electronic voice phenomenon, of what sounded like nefarious laughter. When we played the clip over and over, the file mysteriously deleted itself.

Earlier, a guest I met from New Jersey captured video of what looked like "paranormal darts," or light anomalies that moved around the area where the Borden's privy was located. There have been multiple reports of a sulphur smell in the basement, and it's believed that the house's cellar dweller could be an evil entity. For the record, the group from New Jersey fled the house at 5 a.m. after coming face-to-face with something that terrified them during our investigation.

In addition to my more recent dream involving Bridget Sullivan, I've had spirit communication dreams about the location that began long before I finally visited the haunted crime scene.

In one dream, I see a man wearing 1800s-era clothing and facial hair walking into a house with flowery wallpaper. He takes off his hat and sits on an old-school couch. The dream looks like a black-and-white 35mm and unfolds slower than the typical silent-era film. Before the man can rest his head, he looks at me, and subtitles appear, as if I'm watching a film from the early 1900s. A woman appears holding a hatchet behind her back.

The subtitle that appears in the dream has haunted me for years. It reads: "Diablo did it." Then I wake up.

I didn't figure out the correlation between the house and my dream until I visited the Lizzie Borden House in 2011 while on assignment for a magazine. At that time, I was more interested in trying to solve the murder and was less focused on the message in my dream.

In hindsight, my dream seemed to be implying that the murderer—whether Lizzie, Bridget Sullivan or the uncle John Morse—was possessed by a demonic entity.

Lizzie Borden never shook her "forty whacks" claim to fame. For the record, Borden's stepmother was struck eighteen or nineteen times with a hatchet, and her father suffered eleven blows on the couch. *Photo by Frank C. Grace.*

The crew from *Ghost Adventures* investigated the house in 2011. The most interesting part of the investigation was the paranormal research by Jeff Belanger.

"Andrew and Abby weren't even the first two Bordens to die on that property," Belanger explained. "In 1848, Andrew's uncle lived in the house right next door. His wife went nuts and drowned her three children in a well. One lived. Then she took her own life with a straight razor—slit her throat."

The investigation explored the possibility of an evil entity and the idea that the "property is plagued with dark spirits." I believe this is likely. The electronic voice phenomenon the trio allegedly captured upstairs is terrifying to me. It said: "Keep on killing. Keep 'em coming."

Another message from the spirit box said: "Tell 'em about the girl."

What girl? It's believed that Andrew Borden was communicating a message during the séance and that the message had something to do with the theory, which the psychic medium in *Ghost Adventures* discussed, that the father had an incestuous relationship with Lizzie after her mother, Sarah, died. The girl may have been one of Borden's lesbian lovers.

The uncle, John Morse, testified in court that the night before the murder, Lizzie had had an unidentified guest in her room. He never spotted the mystery guest nor commented on the person's gender.

The murder in 1848 has fueled debate about whether madness ran in the Borden family. In fact, the infanticide by Eliza Darling Borden was actually brought up in

Lizzie's highly publicized trial. It's believed that Eliza drowned her children in the cellar's cistern and then, possibly suffering from postpartum depression, took her own life by cutting her throat with a straight razor.

For the record, Lizzie wasn't a blood relative of Eliza and was connected to her only by marriage through her great-uncle Lawdwick.

The children, who died forty-four years before Abby and Andrew were murdered, are rumored to haunt the land literally next door to the Lizzie Borden House. Guests leave dolls and other toys for ghost children who are believed to inhabit the guest rooms. Children have been heard laughing when no children are present.

During my overnight stay in the Bridget Sullivan room on the third floor, I felt a disembodied hand touch my back. Others have reported that the chair in the room has moved while they were asleep, and the tour guide, Richard Bertoldo, said he has been pushed by an unseen force.

Another explanation for the "tell 'em about the girl" spirit-box message on *Ghost Adventures* is that it could be a reference to the murdered child, Eliza Ann Borden, who was two when she was drowned in the basement of 96 Second St.

In other words, "the girl" the spirit-box message was referring to may be a ghost child. I'm convinced the ghostly resident on the third floor is a little one.

Lee-ann Wilber, manager of the Lizzie Borden House, told the Biography Channel that it's common for guests to run out of the inn in fright. "I'm not used to picking up on things. They just sort of blend in now," Wilber said. "Nothing to drive me out of here."

However, in 2004 she was scared out of the house. She fell asleep on the parlor room's couch and woke at 3 a.m. and saw a shadow person. The old-school chandelier was responsible for the black mist in the hallway, she believed, but she also noticed a misty figure moving up the staircase.

"And as I'm looking at it, it walked up the staircase," Wilber told the Biography Channel. "I said to no one in particular, 'You win tonight,' and went to sleep in my car."

Wilber said she was a skeptic when she moved in more than a decade ago. "Living here," said Wilber, "very quickly, I became a believer."

Because of its gory history, it's no surprise that the Lizzie Borden House is believed to be haunted. Cold spots have been reported numerous times in the master bedroom where Abby came face-to-face with her cold-blooded killer. There's also lore involving a former maid who quit after seeing a body-shaped indentation on the bed in Abby's room.

However, the ghostly reports have turned dark in recent years.

My fear is that the *Ghost Adventures* lockdown may have stirred up negative energy within the house ... or possibly brought in evil from outside the building. According to several sources, the place became unusually active after the investigation.

Currently a bed and breakfast and museum, Borden's house is open for curiosity seekers to spend the night in the actual location where the murders took place. *Photo by Frank C. Grace.*

Rachel Hoffman from Paranormal Xpeditions agreed that the crew of *Ghost Adventures* potentially conjured activity. The paranormal investigator visited the property the day after the *GAC* lockdown. "I went to Lizzie's house and opened the door, and 100 black flies flew out—grown flies," Hoffman explained. "They left six hours before."

Flies—and shadow figures—are common in a home that shelters an evil entity. Nausea, reported by Zak Bagans and Nick Groff on *Ghost Adventures*, is also a reaction to the presence of a dark force. Abby, Andrew, the maid Bridget and even Lizzie herself all reported nausea hours before the two murders in 1892. Temperature fluctuations, specifically in a localized area such as the John Morse room, have been reported in other cases of infestation.

Did Lizzie Borden do it? We'll probably never know for sure. However, if dark forces had been conjured in the house, they may have inspired her to commit the ghastly deed. The devil once roamed here. He's waiting in the shadows of the Lizzie Borden B&B, patiently plotting a return.

Chapter 2

PROVIDENCE BILTMORE
PROVIDENCE, RHODE ISLAND
MOST HAUNTED: #2

"During a blood sacrifice, you're requesting a spirit or entity to come forward. When people conjure something, they think they can contain it ... but they can't. The entity plays to the human's requests, but it's controlling your every step."

—James Annitto, demonologist and founder of the Dominion Ministry

In 2015, I received a mysterious package in the mail from an anonymous source in the United Kingdom. It was an envelope containing an old-school hotel room key and an odd note: "Hope you enjoy your stay." The aqua-colored key looked like it was from the 1960s or earlier and was marked "The Biltmore Hotel & Motor Inn." It had a Providence, Rhode Island address, and I was immediately hit with a wave of emotion when I held the key in my hand.

As a psychometrist, I'm sometimes able to pick up on lingering energy from haunted objects. The key had an intense psychic imprint involving a young lady and a sailor. In the vision, I was overwhelmed with emotions relating to a woman waiting in a hotel room for the man she loved. Perhaps he went to war and never returned? She kept returning to the hotel room and made him promise that he would come back for her. He never returned.

I kept the key in a drawer at home, and, in many ways, it inspired me to write *13 Most Haunted Hotels & Inns of New England*. I had no idea the key would lead me to one of the most haunted hotels in New England and would unlock a floodgate of spiritual energy still lingering in the halls of this extremely haunted and historic hotel.

The Providence Biltmore opened on June 6, 1922 and boasts an almost too-good-to-be-true past that rivals some of pop culture's more infamous hotels. In fact, it's often said to be the inspiration for the Overlook in Stephen King's *The Shining* and the Bates Motel in *Psycho*.

A hotel where guests check in but don't check out? Yes, the Providence Biltmore has that notorious reputation.

Located on the southern corner of Kennedy Plaza at 11 Dorrance St. in downtown Providence, Rhode Island, the Providence Biltmore has been named "America's Most Haunted Hotel" by the American Hotel & Lodging Association. *Photo by Jason Baker.*

The Beaux-Arts style building located at 11 Dorrance St. in downtown Providence was designed by the team, Warren and Wetmore, who also built Grand Central Terminal in Manhattan. The hotel was a Sheraton-owned structure for years, and it was flooded in 1954 after Hurricane Carol decimated the Ocean State. In fact, there's a plaque in the Providence Biltmore lobby demarcating the flood waters, which reached almost eight feet during the 1950s-era storm.

Named "America's Most Haunted Hotel" in 2000 by the American Hotel & Lodging Association, the Providence Biltmore was allegedly financed by practicing Satanist Johan Leisse Weisskopf, who supposedly wanted to showcase his religion to New England's not-so-puritanical denizens. The original design included a poultry farm on the roof with a working chicken coop. According to a far-fetched legend, the fowl were sacrificed in a blood ritual, and the basement was used for purification ceremonies.

The second floor was home to the scantily-clad Bacchante Girls, who paraded around the Garden Room and served luminaries such as Douglas Fairbanks, F. Scott and Zelda Fitzgerald and Louis Armstrong. Because of its naughty reputation and Weisskopf's ties to the Rhode Island mafia, the Providence Biltmore became a hotbed of nefarious activity during the Prohibition era, and a series of murders and sexual assaults are said to have occurred at the grand hotel from 1920 to 1933, including a horrific drowning involving an eleven-year-old prostitute in one of the room's bathtubs.

"Among the hauntings reported, the sound of raucous parties has been heard by guests for decades, as well as locked doors suddenly unlocking, the sound of laughter and moving orbs, especially on the sixteenth floor, as well as the apparition of a female spirit," reported Robert A. Geake in *Historic Taverns of Rhode Island*. "In his book, *Haunted Providence*, mentalist Rory Raven also reports sightings of an unfortunate stockbroker who plunged to his death from the fourteenth floor on Black Tuesday in 1929. The room where he stayed is reportedly haunted, and guests are sometimes startled by the unsettling vision of a man falling past their windows to the street below."

When I booked my overnight stay at this notoriously haunted hotel, I intuitively knew it was going to be one helluva night. In fact, I read that the Providence Biltmore has a reputation for guests going missing under mysterious circumstances. One reported case of people vanishing from the hotel was as recent as 2008. I sheepishly warned my friends to send out a search party if they didn't hear from me.

The lobby, which resembles Grand Central Terminal in New York City, oozed a "something wicked this way comes" vibe. Courtney, the spunky, front-desk concierge at the Providence Biltmore, said she technically hadn't had any firsthand encounters with ghosts at the hotel. However, she does often retell guests a story from her first day on the job at the historic haunt. "I was nervous about working at what was supposedly one of the most haunted hotels in New England," she told me. "During my first night at the hotel, I walked into one of the empty rooms with the lights out, and I saw what looked like a shadow figure reflected in the mirror. The dark mass was in the shape of a person. When I turned on the lights, I realized it was me. It was my reflection."

The concierge jokingly said she fabricated the story. However, I wasn't convinced it was totally made up. When Courtney recounted the tall tale, she had fear in her eyes.

One of the more notorious ghosts said to haunt the Providence Biltmore is a Depression-era financier who lost all his money in 1929 and jumped from the hotel's fourteenth floor. *Photo by Frank C. Grace.*

My room was on the twelfth floor and was in the "drop zone" of the man who plunged to his death in 1929. According to reports, the residual energy haunts all the rooms he passes. As far as the residual haunting is concerned, it's almost like a videotaped replay of a traumatic event that occurred years ago.

On the second floor, outside of the former Bacchante Room, I met with demonologist James Annitto and his paranormal friend Russ Stiver. We were focused on the symbols scattered throughout the Providence Biltmore's ornate lobby, which featured a recurring sphinx motif and an urn. So many labyrinthine rooms and secret entrances surrounded us, we almost got lost in what seemed like a maze of haunted history. Both Annitto and Stiver felt a heavy presence on the mezzanine level.

After taking a trip to the top floor, which had a past life as a chicken coop, the twenty-seven-year-old demonologist and I talked about the rumored animal sacrifices that had occurred in the hotel. "Most blood rituals are bad news," Annitto told me. "During a blood sacrifice, you're requesting a spirit or entity to come forward. When people conjure something, they think they can contain it …

but they can't. The entity plays to the human's requests, but it's controlling your every step. The blood ritual creates a fundamental energy shift at a location, and it amplifies the haunting."

Stiver is an empath. He talked about the large number of unreported suicides and deaths he sensed had occurred at the hotel. "Sordid activities have left an imprint on the building," he said. "When you walk into this place, you immediately feel the heaviness."

During our discussion on the historic second floor, Stiver felt a spirit lurking over his shoulder. "I'm getting a middle-aged gentleman. The hotel was a playground for people, and he came here on business ... but it was definitely for pleasure," Stiver emoted.

The demonologist agreed with the empath. "There is so much history in Providence and specifically at this hotel," Annitto said nervously, looking over Stiver's shoulder. "I'm in construction, and when you start building a hotel like the Providence Biltmore, deaths happen. I bet many people have died here and that includes all of the unreported deaths and suicides that have happened in this hotel over the past century."

I jokingly called the Providence Biltmore "suicide central," and when I glanced up, I saw what looked like a lady in white dart past the entrance to the second floor's State Room. I initially called her a "flapper ghost," but in hindsight she looked more like she was from the late 1930s or early 1940s. We quickly gathered our belongings and followed the spirit down several hallways that led us to a wall display of historical artifacts.

In one of the photos, showcased among other hotel ephemera, there seemed to be a group of sailors and women enjoying one last night together before the men headed overseas. The photo oddly reminded me of the final scene from *The Shining* when viewers realize that the film's contemporary antagonist, Jack Torrance, is somehow in the photo from a New Year's Eve bash at the Overlook Hotel in 1921.

I told Annitto and Stiver about the key I'd received in the mail, and I immediately received a spirit communication from the ghost lady in the hallway begging me to take a closer look at the photo. I looked again at the historic picture and saw a woman in white. She looked upset. She was sitting next to a sailor, and it seemed that the men were about to head off to war. Based on the room's decor in the picture, it was a celebration of sorts, possibly a dance.

Was the lady in white luring me to the hotel so she could tell me her story? Was the key I'd mysteriously received in the mail in 2015 somehow related to the full-bodied apparition I'd spotted on the second floor?

In the wee hours of the night, after Annitto and Stiver had left, I returned to the State Room area where I'd encountered the lady in white. I walked down the long corridor with my EVP recorder in hand. My goal was to communicate with the spirit again and hopefully get some answers.

When I approached the hallway with the glass-encased photo, a security guard popped out of nowhere and politely told me that the area was off limits to guests.

He locked the door, and I wasn't able to access the artifacts hidden in the hotel's corridor of secrets.

Last dance at the Providence Biltmore? I will probably never know for sure what happened to the lady in white. However, based on my sleepless night at this extremely haunted hotel in Providence, the hotel's Prohibition-era party continues in the afterlife.

Chapter 3

CAPTAIN GRANT'S INN
PRESTON, CONNECTICUT
MOST HAUNTED: #3

"The main ghost was Adelaide who was Captain Grant's wife. I had a lot of conversations with her so I'm happy that she crossed over. She had been waiting around for Captain Grant for a long, long time."

—Carol Matsumoto, innkeeper and author of "The Ghosts of Captain Grant's Inn"

Nestled between Connecticut's Foxwoods and Mohegan Sun casinos, Preston's 1754 Captain Grant's Inn is a ghost hunter's version of winning the lottery. Based on a recent visit to the historic inn, I accidentally stumbled upon one of New England's most haunted—and most eccentric—overnight haunts.

Listed on the National Register of Historic Places, Captain Grant's Inn was built in 1754 and is part of Connecticut's Poquetanuck Village. Nearby is a cove that leads out to the Thames River and eventually the Atlantic Ocean. "This is the cove where Captain William Grant set sail for Honduras laden with grist to be traded for Mahogany," claimed the inn's website.

One of my readers suggested I visit Captain Grant's Inn based on the location's haunted history. "The house is filled with energy, being built in 1754," explained Samantha Brittany. "I got orb pictures and had some strange unexplainable things happened, and we were able to visit the graveyard in the backyard. Captain Grant is buried across the street in another cemetery, so there's one graveyard in the front and one in back of the house, full of wandering spirits."

Carol Matsumoto, who runs the historic inn with her husband Ted, confirmed the haunted shenanigans within the structure. In fact, she recently wrote a book called *The Ghosts of Captain Grant's Inn: True Stories from a Haunted Connecticut Inn*. "The hauntings have been going on from the very beginning since we purchased the place," said Matsumoto, who purchased and then renovated the property in the mid-1990s. "The main ghost was Adelaide, who was Captain Grant's wife," she continued, claiming that Adelaide's spirit recently left the building. "I had a lot of conversations with her, so I'm happy that she crossed over. She had been waiting around for Captain Grant for a long, long time."

Innkeeper Carol Matsumoto wrote a book called *The Ghosts of Captain Grant's Inn* in which she recounted her experiences of the overnight haunt's spirits. *Photo by Sam Baltrusis.*

Adelaide, also known as Mercy, lived in the Grant homestead well into her eighties. During the Revolutionary War, soldiers from the Continental Army were stationed there, and during the Civil War, escaped slaves were sheltered on the property. "There's a lot of female energy here, and there's slave energy here as well," explained Matsumoto. "The field, which is our back lawn, is where the Native Americans met with the Dutch, and it's where they traded goods. The field has been heavily dug up with people looking for artifacts."

Several TV shows filmed at Captain Grant's Inn, including A&E's *Psychic Kids*, the Travel Channel's *Most Terrifying Places in America* and *Dig Wars*.

The inn boasts a three-story porch and six working fireplaces, but the most haunted spot in the building is reportedly the Adelaide room.

"One guest claims to have awakened in the middle of the night to see next to her bed a woman dressed in Colonial-era garb, holding hands with two children. There have also been claims of the TV turning itself on and off as well as the shower curtain being knocked down without provocation," reported the website *Damned Connecticut*. "Some visitors have reported hearing random knockings and seeing unusual shapes. One guest described the sensation of having her face caressed by invisible hands; another told of the shadow of a young child passing through them. Paranormal investigators have also allegedly recorded EVPs here, including the voice of a young girl. Phantom footsteps have been heard in the attic."

Matsumoto claimed that the inn also has a resident gay ghost. "When they were filming *Dig Wars*, one of the participants was staying in the Adelaide room. He had this vivid dream of this gorgeous woman, and when he woke up, there was a ghost on top of him. He came down, shaking. I think that ghost was Liam, our gay ghost. He lived in the 1700s," the innkeeper explained.

The author and innkeeper, who tapped into her ability to connect with the spirit realm later in life using dowsing rods, said she confronted Liam's spirit after the incident. "I had a hard time talking to him. He died in his twenties, and it was an accident," she recalled. "I found out he was gay when I asked him who he liked in the room, and it was only the men. I asked him if he was made fun of, and he said he was."

Poquetanuck's first cemetery is also located behind the inn. Based on my personal experience, the burial ground seemed to be the vortex of the property's paranormal activity. After checking out the cemetery twice, I fell into a deep sleep at Captain Grant's Inn. It's as if my energy was drained ... and the spirits wanted to connect with me in a meditative state. I did dream of a little girl ghost who connected with me immediately.

Even though my friend and I were not staying in what has been reported to be the most haunted room, we were not alone. The Ovilus spewed out words like "little" when I asked who was with us. I also asked who else was in the room, and the device said "writer." I asked where I should go next, and the Ovilus said "grave."

Each room at the inn has a book with notes from previous guests. We stayed in the Collette Room, and, to be honest, the stories creeped me out. "The first night I woke up suddenly, feeling as if someone was standing next to the bed only to find my shoes had been moved. On my second night, I awoke to the sound of someone breathing in my ear. Mr. Whipple made his presence known around midnight-ish, as he stomped through the parlor while we were quietly sitting," wrote one guest in 2012.

Another family who stayed in the room mentioned a little girl spirit known as Deborah Adams. "As for the spirits that also reside here, we were happy that we had such great encounters with orbs in the Adelaide room and that a little girl Deborah actually communicated with us," the guest wrote. Another person wrote, "I experienced a little girl on the right side of my bed."

After a face-to-face encounter with a young child spirit in the wee hours of the night, I asked Matsumoto about Deborah Adams the following morning at breakfast. Apparently, former guests have also had experiences of the little girl ghost, whom some have described as wearing pigtails. According to the innkeeper, one woman was determined to find the young girl's final resting spot. "They wanted to see if they could find her grave," Matsumoto explained over breakfast. "At that time, the weeds and briars were knee-high. You couldn't even walk in the graveyard."

Some of the ghosts lingering in Captain Grant's Inn are buried in the creepy cemetery nestled behind the haunted B&B in Preston, Connecticut. *Photo by Frank C. Grace.*

Matsumoto continued, "So we got a weed whacker, and the woman who saw Deborah Adams took the dowsing rods and led the way. There was a whole procession of us going across the field. The dowsing rods were guiding us, and we eventually did find her grave. I came back to the house and prayed. Oddly, when we went back out into the cemetery to find Deborah's grave again … it was gone. We haven't been able to find her marker since that first encounter."

In hindsight, a few things happened during my overnight stay at Captain Grant's Inn. My shoes were mysteriously moved sometime during the night. In fact, I noticed that I was missing one of my black shoes when my friend and I were waiting for our bus at Foxwoods. Ted Matsumoto, who owns the historic inn with Carol, found the shoe hidden beneath a table and dropped it off to me before our bus left.

Do I think the ghost girl moved my shoe? Yes.

I was also missing an important protection stone given to me at the S.K. Pierce Victorian Mansion in Gardner, Massachusetts. It was on the nightstand next to me while I was sleeping. I took it out of my pocket after I saw what looked like a ghost girl wearing a bonnet next to the bed. Yes, the spirit has my protection rock. I'm hoping little Deborah Adams has it stored somewhere in the extremely haunted Captain Grant's Inn and will somehow return it to me during my next overnight stay.

Looking for a room with a "boo" in Connecticut? Head to Preston's Captain Grant's Inn hidden between Foxwoods and Mohegan Sun casinos. The haunted hotspot's resident spirits are dying to have you stay.

Chapter 4

ORLEANS WATERFRONT INN
CAPE COD, MASSACHUSETTS
MOST HAUNTED: #4

"My wife says don't upset the ghosts. We look at it as Hannah's inn. It's her home and we take care of it for her."

—Ed Maas, co-owner of the Orleans Waterfront Inn

I'm doing an overnight at the allegedly haunted Orleans Waterfront Inn on July Fourth weekend in Cape Cod. Oddly, the fireworks are happening *inside* this historic structure built in 1875. I somehow chose the haunted spot, which is Room 5. Unbeknownst to me at the time, my bed for the night made a recent cameo on an episode of Syfy's *Ghost Hunters*.

"Built in 1875, the inn was initially a hardware store and was then renovated into a speakeasy run by the Irish mob, as well as a bordello," reported *MassLive* in a recap of the 2010 TAPS investigation. "There was a murder on the premises. One of the prostitutes was found dead outside of the inn. Various other apparitions were reported, including two of the workers who committed suicide, both by hanging, on the premises and a naked woman dancing in the lobby."

I purposely don't do research before going to a supposedly haunted location. When I booked the hotel, I liked the room's name, which is simply "1875," a hat tip to the year it was built. Of course, I chose the suite where guests check in but refuse to check out. Yes, according to reports, two women, who were "not right," once refused to leave the room on their own accord. Employees at the inn claimed they would hear what sounded like an animal growling and possibly a foreign language that sounded like German when one woman barricaded herself inside the second-floor locale.

"We are also told about the history of Room 5 where not one but two women checked in for a weekend and then stayed for about five months, only being removed forcefully from the rooms, one by family, one by the police," reported MassLive.

It was only after purchasing the property that Ed Maas discovered that the Orleans Waterfront Inn was haunted. *Photo by Frank C. Grace.*

Owner Ed Maas, who purchased the haunted hotel in 1996, wrote about the room in his book *Ghost of the Orleans Inn*. He believes the room's haunting relates to the reported suicide of a German visitor in the inn's downstairs bathroom.

"Although the cause of death may have been determined, it is unclear of the manner. If it was by knife, was the owner of it perhaps escorted away from the scene? There is little information about the death, and little is ever spoken of it," Maas wrote. "The room above the restroom is particularly interesting. Guests check in for a short stay and seem unwilling to leave. One particular guest exhibited multiple personalities as a German SS soldier. To hear the German's cursing coming from the elderly female was frightening. It seemed as if German interrogations were going on behind closed doors."

Within the first hour of my stay, I chatted with the owner's daughter, Meaghan, who gave me a brief walk-through of the location, which has been featured on Syfy's *Ghost Hunters* and in various paranormal books. In the lobby, a "hidden room" once housed bootlegged liquor and provided cover for various other underworld activities during its Irish mobster-era heyday. Meaghan told me about the history of my room and recounted the story of how two previous guests had refused to leave. "It's definitely a room with a strange history," she joked, struggling to unlock the door. "You should definitely visit the cupola upstairs before it gets dark."

Within the first hour, I went to the top floor and read a letter to "Hannah," the resident spirit of the 1875 inn. I carried an Ovilus with me as I walked through the hotel's belvedere and then creeped up into the cupola. The air in the small room overlooking Orleans's Town Cove felt psychically charged, as if something horrible had happened there. With the Ovilus, I picked up "with" when I asked if the spirit was with us. It also said "Jones" and "devil" when I asked who had murdered the inn's resident ghost.

I had an intense reaction in the cupola, as if the spirit in the room wanted to communicate with me. It was a male energy, and the spirit box kept spitting out words like "rubber" and "sex." In fact, the novelty investigation tool spewed out words so fast, I had to turn it off. The spirit seemed sexually charged and somewhat misogynistic. I didn't know it at the time, but the cupola is where the bartender, Fred, had hanged himself in the 1950s.

The cupola is also where Steve Gonsalves from *Ghost Hunters* picked up an EVP that sounded like "let me out." However, Gonsalves believed it said "get me down."

When Mark Jasper wrote about the Orleans Waterfront Inn in *Haunted Cape Cod*, he appropriately named the chapter on the inn "Gangsters & Ghosts."

"The house was originally built in 1875 by Aaron Snow II for his wife and seven children," wrote Jasper. "He was a direct descendant of Constance Hopkins, who was the first person to spot Cape Cod from the Mayflower as it sailed near Eastham in 1620. Hannah and Fred are thought to be the two ghosts responsible for some of the bizarre incidents that have transpired in the inn over the years.

Unsure of the identities of the murdered prostitutes, the Maases named the female ghost Hannah. Fred, you recall, was the bartender who hanged himself in the cupola. Hannah apparently loves to play with doors."

She also apparently loves to play with paranormal researchers. My overnight stay in this extremely haunted hotel was terrifyingly memorable. As I was sitting on the bed and reaching for my computer, I felt something rub up against my leg. I told my friend about the bizarre sensation. It turns out the inn has a history of "ghost cats," specifically in the neighboring Room 4.

I also captured an EVP outside of the inn that still haunts me. I was sitting on a bench near the 300-year-old Jonathan Young windmill, and I had what I can only describe as a psychic moment in which I relived what I believe to be the murder of the young woman who still lingers in the inn. Based on my vision, she was in love with one of her suitors, and he shot her because she knew too much. I have no idea what the vision means, except that she was completely not expecting to be shot outside of the structure known as "Aaron's Folly" by a man she was courting.

During the EVP session, I asked the spirit if she was murdered. I picked up what sounded like a whispering female—a whispering that got progressively louder as the recording continued. When I asked her to tell me her name, I clearly picked up what sounded like either "Anna" or "Hannah." I was in shock. I quickly packed up my things and went inside. I thought about leaving the haunted Orleans Inn after that eerie EVP session. However, I was scheduled to interview the owner the following morning.

One of the first things Ed Maas heard from the locals after he purchased the historic Orleans Waterfront Inn in 1996 is that the property is notoriously haunted and that it would be in his best interests not to upset the ghosts.

When asked if he knew the Orleans Inn was haunted before he purchased it, Maas shook his head. "I had no idea," he told me. "I had driven by the inn for twenty-five years and never came inside. It was slated to be knocked down, and I wasn't told by the realtor. After we purchased it, I then found out that the inn was written about in the *Cape Cod Times*, and I called the realtor and asked them about it, and I quickly learned the inn was rumored to be haunted. We then made ourselves comfortable with the ghosts."

Maas initially shrugged off the spirited stories until he had a face-to-face encounter with the female apparition of a ghost he now calls Hannah. "When we bought the inn, I would stay here around the clock. At midnight, I would lie on the couch to get some sleep. In the middle of the night, I saw what I thought was one of the guests come downstairs stark naked. I said 'hello,' and she 'hello' back. I didn't think much of it until a woman stopped her car outside of the inn a few days later after seeing a naked woman dancing in the fifth floor belvedere. That's when I put two and two together."

The owner said he had his first encounter with Hannah in 2000. When I asked him if he'd had any experiences with the ghosts outside the property, he quickly told me that that's where she'd been killed.

25

"Hannah was murdered outside," he explained. "We believe she lived in Room 5, but most of the sightings have been in Room 4. In fact, we just had a group record an EVP session with Hannah, and they asked her if she was happy, and she said she was. During the Roaring Twenties, this was a house of ill-repute. We believe the spirit is the woman who was murdered here in the 1920s."

Maas, the father of eight children, said his family is at peace with the inn's resident spirits. "We don't tell the guests about the ghosts before they check in," he continued. "Some people know about it, and some come here specifically for the hauntings. It's not something that we really promote. My wife says, 'don't upset the ghosts.' We look at it as Hannah's inn. It's her home, and we take care of it for her."

Chapter 5

OMNI MOUNT WASHINGTON
BRETTON WOODS, NEW HAMPSHIRE
MOST HAUNTED: #5

"It really did remind me of the Overlook Hotel from 'The Shining' with its long silent corridors and beautiful old architecture."

—Peter Muise, author and founder of the "New England Folklore" blog

Traveling through New Hampshire's White Mountains feels magical, as if one is being transported back in time. Established in 1918, the White Mountain National Forest boasts 1,225 square miles and includes two dozen Paleo-Indian sites dating back thousands of years. The land, once considered sacred by New Hampshire's Native population, wasn't settled by colonists until after the Revolutionary War and eventually became a vacation hotspot for tourists in the nineteenth century.

Mount Washington, which tops 6,288 feet and is the highest peak in northeastern North America, was nicknamed "Agiocochook" by the region's Native Americans. They refused to climb to the top of it because they believed the summit was home to the Great Spirit. Of course, this didn't stop people like Sylvester Marsh, who built the so-called "railway to the moon" in the late 1860s. His creation was the world's first rack-and-pinion railroad. Believe it or not, the Mount Washington Cog Railway is still in operation today, and the mountain-climbing train is celebrating its 150-year anniversary in 2019.

It should come as no surprise that New Hampshire's majestic Mount Washington is home to one of New England's most haunted hotels.

Construction of the Mount Washington Hotel kicked off in 1900 and was completed on July 28, 1902. The largest wooden building in New England, the hotel was the brainchild of Joseph Stickney, a wealthy industrialist who made his money in coal and the railroads. Unfortunately, he didn't get to enjoy his Spanish Renaissance Revival hotel very long. Stickney died only one year after it opened to the public.

Construction on the Mount Washington Hotel began in 1900 and was completed in 1902. *Photo by Frank C. Grace.*

However, it's not Stickney but his wife Carolyn who's believed to watch over the guests of the Omni Mount Washington—even in the afterlife. Known as the "princess," she remarried a European prince shortly after Joseph's death and enjoyed spending her summers at the hotel. "She built a private dining room for her and her friends and also had a special balcony constructed that overlooked the hotel's main dining room," explained author Peter Muise. "This allowed her to see what other guests were wearing and change her clothes to ensure she was the best dressed woman in the room."

Muise, who chronicled his visit to the Omni Mount Washington on his *New England Folklore* blog, said staff at the hotel started to report ghostly happenings after Carolyn died in 1936. "During the empty winter months, caretakers claimed they saw an elegant woman walking into the dining room and that lights would turn themselves on and off," Muise wrote. "When a posed photo of the summer staff was developed, a shadowy woman could be seen looking at them through a window, but no one had been at the window when the photo was taken."

For those looking for a spine-tingling overnight stay, Muise told me that the best time to visit the hotel is during the off-season months. "Foliage season was over and ski season hadn't yet begun and the roads were really empty as we drove up from Boston," he said. "A lot of the businesses we passed were closed for the season so things felt extra spooky. We arrived after dark and as we drove up the long driveway we could see this massive old building all lit up against the night. The hotel really has a lot of presence."

The *Legends and Lore of the North Shore* author said New Hampshire's Bretton Woods becomes a literal ghost town in November. "There weren't a lot of other guests staying there so the place was pretty quiet," Muise remembered. "It really did remind me of the Overlook Hotel from *The Shining* with its long silent corridors and beautiful old architecture."

Did Muise encounter Stickney's ghost? No. However, he has heard several creepy stories about the hotel over the years. In fact, Muise said one of his family members was freaked out by the hotel's ghosts when she worked at a conference there. "Lots of supplies and materials kept disappearing and moving around, which she thought was kind of strange," Muise told me. "She also said that when a friend of hers stayed in Room 314, the famous haunted room, the lights kept turning themselves on and off, and the shower would run when no one was there."

My friend Lucky Belcamino, the official psychic-medium of the Lizzie Borden B&B, said the hotel's ghostly inhabitants don't necessarily come out on command. "I do believe that the hotel has lingering spirits, residual energies and hidden secrets," explained Belcamino, who recently investigated the historic hotel. "I was picking up on some impressions that there were a few spirits interested in my energy while I stayed there and walked the halls and property. Being on a different level of energy when I do my mediumship, I'm sure they are attracted to the higher vibration, so they were trying to make a connection to me."

Belcamino told me a male energy lingers near Room 13, and her team picked up several words such as "food" and "fun" on a spirit box. "We definitely were communicating with a male, and he seems to stick around, although he was not giving us much information," the psychic-medium explained. "I also believe and felt that there were many entities lingering on the property not specific to male or female."

According to Thomas D'Agostino, author of *Haunted New England*, the full-bodied apparition of a woman wearing fine Victorian dress, believed to be Carolyn Stickney, has been spotted gliding down the hotel's hallways. "Guests have heard a slight rap on their door, and upon answering it, they found no one there," he wrote. "The most active of all rooms is number 314. This is where the princess's hand-turned maple bed now resides. Many guests have been roused from a sound sleep by the sensation of someone sitting on the edge of the bed."

Looking for a room with a "boo" in New Hampshire? Take the mountain-climbing cog train to the extremely haunted Omni Mount Washington. Apparently, the hotel's staff of ghostly inhabitants will treat you like a princess even in the afterlife.

Chapter 6

LONGFELLOW'S WAYSIDE INN
SUDBURY, MASSACHUSETTS
MOST HAUNTED: #6

"We recorded crying on a device that only records electromagnetic fields. It blew our mind because it was someone balling."

—Michael Baker, Para-Boston investigator

Jerusha Howe, the resident wailing spirit of Longfellow's Wayside Inn, was known as the Belle of Sudbury. She's also said to have died in 1842 from a broken heart. Her legend, which was immortalized by the alpha-male paranormal investigation team from the Travel Channel's *Ghost Adventures*, has morphed over the years.

However, one story has been consistent. The ghostly woman is said to haunt both Room 9, her old bed chamber, and Room 10, which is believed to be where she sewed.

For the record, Longfellow's Wayside Inn was built in 1716. Originally called Howe Tavern, it was renamed after Henry Wadsworth Longfellow visited the historic hotspot with his publisher James Fields in October 1862. Longfellow penned the book *Tales of a Wayside Inn* in 1863.

Jerusha was the oldest sister of the last Howe innkeeper, Lyman, who was known as "the squire" back in the 1800s. "She was well educated, well dressed and loved to paint and read and sing to the guests and visitors of the inn," explained former innkeeper John Cowden to WBZ-TV. "People want this room because of the history with Jerusha. Its ambiance, dark paneling and plank flooring," the innkeeper explained, adding that there's a Secret Drawer Society allowing guests to leave notes of what they experienced in Room 9.

According to Cowden, guests claim they hear Howe playing her piano and her footsteps in the night. The innkeeper told WBZ-TV that he's never encountered the ghosts of Longfellow's Wayside Inn. "I have not experienced them myself, but because we heard so many, you just don't know," he continued.

The man who ditched Howe promised to come back to Sudbury to continue their courtship, but he never did. Born in 1797, she died at forty-five, unmarried and heartbroken.

The ghost of Jerusha Howe is rumored to haunt Longfellow's Wayside Inn in Sudbury. *Photo by Frank C. Grace.*

What happened to her beloved? "Little is known of Jerusha's romantic affairs in life, but as the story goes, she was engaged to an Englishman," explained Alyson Horrocks in *Yankee Magazine*. "The legend claims that he sailed home to England to make arrangements for the wedding and was never heard from again. There has been speculation that he drowned at sea, or he simply abandoned her, and perhaps he never existed at all."

According to *Ghost Adventures* front man Zak Bagans, Jerusha is "America's most amorous female ghost," and he felt her spirit was teasing him during the paranormal investigation or "lockdown," making Bagans want more.

"Longfellow's Wayside Inn is home to America's most romantic haunt," announced Bagans on the February 2011 Travel Channel episode. "The ghost of a woman who still pines away waiting for her lover to return from across the sea is experienced throughout the building. It is said that she only focuses on the men who sleep in her bedroom."

In the episode, Bagans continued to sexualize the dead woman's postmortem pleas for the British visitor she fell in love with in the early 1840s. Bagans jokingly surmised that "guests have had intimate encounters with Jerusha" and announced his intentions to "hook up" with the female spirit at Longfellow's Wayside Inn. "Sorry everybody to bug your Valentine's Day dinner," Bagans awkwardly said from the dinner table. "I do have something I would like to say. There's a spirit of a woman who is very beautiful. She's gorgeous, and that's who I'm going to hook up with."

Bagans interviewed Dan Grillo, a regular overnight guest who stays in the notoriously haunted Room 9. Grillo said he had a face-to-face encounter with Jerusha's ghost, adding that "it wasn't sexual. It was comforting." The spirit allegedly only appears to men, even when the man's wife is sharing the bed.

"It was two in the morning," recalled Grillo. "An arm went around me and went across my back, and I was like, 'who is this?' I jumped up at the side of the bed. It was a clear impression."

Was it Jerusha? "Oh yeah," Grillo responded. "Other people I've talked to say they've seen her standing in the corner."

Bagan's investigation produced some compelling evidence. He claimed to have seen a ghostly dress sway near Jerusha's room, although it wasn't captured on camera. The team did film a misty form with a distinct head using a full-spectrum camera. They also experienced female cries, mysterious tapping, temperature fluctuations and doors slamming in both Room 9 and 10. Bagans claimed that Jerusha put her icy-cold hands on his knees and that the spirit played with his belt. After the lockdown, Bagans spent a night alone in Howe's room to get to know her better. Fellow castmates Nick Groff and Aaron Goodwin joked that Bagans had a "ghost fetish."

Wayside Inn's Old Bar room is the oldest room in the historic structure. It was the first-floor chamber of David Howe's 1707 two-room homestead and became a watering hole called Howe's Tavern in 1716 and eventually Red Horse Tavern. *Photo by Frank C. Grace.*

Based purely on the special Valentine's Day *Ghost Adventures* episode, Howe is a sex-crazed succubus. Michael Baker, founder of the scientific group called the New England Center for the Advancement of Paranormal Science (NECAPS) and lead investigator with Para-Boston, said Bagans painted an over-the-top and somewhat misogynistic portrait of Wayside Inn's resident ghost.

Howe is heartbroken over an unrequited love affair. Based on Baker's exhaustive research, she possibly left a psychic imprint from her emotional breakdown when the Englishman didn't respond to her letters.

Apparently, the cliché "hell hath no fury like a woman scorned" also applies in the afterlife.

"That *Ghost Adventures* episode is horrendous," responded Baker. "We have captured a lot of evidence at the Wayside Inn over the years. It started with a knock on the door. The entire group heard it and looked at the door, and we recorded it. We opened the door right away, and no one was there. The stairs outside are narrow, curved and extremely creaky. No one could have knocked on that door and got away that fast unheard."

Baker's "real science, real answers" mantra cuts through the usual smoke and mirrors associated with the "Boo!" business. With Baker, there's no over-the-top *Ghostbusters* gear or fake Cockney accents. When it comes to science-based paranormal investigations, Baker is the real deal.

"Basically, there is no ghost-catching device," explained Baker. "The field has changed. It has taken more of a funhouse approach—it has become a novelty—and it has set the paranormal investigation field back in a way. A lot of people are trying to use a screwdriver to hammer a nail. People go in with preconceived notions, and if anything happens, they're going to come to a certain conclusion. If something moves, bumps or they hear footsteps, they're going to automatically assume that it's a ghost, and that's a bad way to investigate."

Baker continued: "Technology can't detect spirits … We have to prove that spirits exist before we can build anything that can measure them. There was a shift in the field, occurring in the '90s, where it's a game to mimic what is seen on television. There was a period where it was purely scientific, and now people think they can turn off the lights, pick up an infrared camera and capture a ghost."

Baker said Longfellow's Wayside Inn is arguably the most active location he's investigated. "We recorded a video of a shadow coming out of the floor twice. The first time it came out of the floor and back down, and the next time it flew over the bed. This video confirmed the location of guest sightings. Then I recorded someone fumbling on a piano at 4 a.m. It wasn't a song. It was fumbling, and it lasted twenty minutes. Jerusha's piano is there, but it doesn't work and is in the museum at the other end of the inn. It was audible to the ears, and I couldn't hear it outside the room. Jerusha used to play that piano in her room."

The paranormal investigator said Howe's cries were captured on tape. "We recorded crying on a device that only records electromagnetic fields. It was captured in the same area as the shadow. It blew our mind because it was someone balling," he explained.

"That same night, the hot water in the bathroom turned on by itself. We had cameras running in the room while we ate dinner. When we returned from dinner, the water in the bathroom had turned on. We could hear the water running on our recordings. We listened to the recordings when the last person used the bathroom, and no water was heard. So something turned the water on full blast while we left the room. The bathroom is also in the same area as the shadow."

Baker, who's normally Para-Boston's skeptic, said he believes that Longfellow's Wayside Inn is one of the most haunted locations in Massachusetts. "I'm convinced because each time these things occurred, they happened with strict controls and monitoring of the environment," Baker continued. "There was no obvious explanation, and these things should not have been possible. They shouldn't have occurred, but they did."

The paranormal investigator said the Wayside Inn's ghost lore extends beyond Jerusha. "There was a sighting at the end of the 1800s of a half-body woman walking through what is now the ballroom. It left such an impression that they renamed the room the Hobgoblin Room.

According to Brian E. Plumb's *A History of Longfellow's Wayside Inn*, "a woman of the Howe family [long ago] claimed she saw a ghost floating, half running through this room on a dark night." The Hobgoblin Room, once called the Old Hall, was rechristened in 1868 after the historic ghost sighting.

Baker and his team have spent months scanning and transcribing letters from the Secret Drawer Society, which chronicle guests' encounters with Howe's ghost. A tradition dating to 1990 but believed to have started in 1923, the notes are kept in the nooks and crannies of Jerusha's room. "The best part about them is it's unsolicited testimony," concluded Baker. "Nobody asked those people if they had a paranormal experience. The experience itself moved them to write those notes."

Hundreds of letters are kept in Baker's database. One note, written on New Year's Day in 2006, talked about an encounter with Jerusha in the wee hours of the night on January 1. "They say you only appear to men, but both my wife and I heard you," wrote one anonymous guest. "After seeing a jagged beam of white light and hearing your strange knocking, we managed to drift back to sleep. You have made us question our beliefs in the supernatural and the structure of life. Your presence has confirmed for us that we are not alone."

Chapter 7

PILGRIM HOUSE INN
NEWPORT, RHODE ISLAND
MOST HAUNTED: #7

"It's 2 a.m., and I can hear what sounds like a girl sobbing in the next room. There are no kids here with us at the Pilgrim House Inn. She sounds so scared."

—Sam Baltrusis, notes from the Pilgrim House Inn's Room 8

If you're looking for a truly haunted New England experience, visit Rhode Island's Newport during the off-season months. My first trip to the creepy summer vacation hotspot was November 2015, and I was on a quest to visit a cemetery in nearby Portsmouth, Rhode Island. The Irish-Catholic burial ground was the final resting spot for my newly uncovered ancestors, who lived in the "City by the Sea" in the late 1600s. Also, I've always wanted to visit the beautiful Bellevue Avenue mansions, which served as "summer cottages" for America's rich and famous during the Gilded Age.

During my post-Halloween visit, Newport was a literal "ghost town" in more ways than one.

The bus from Boston dropped my skeptic friend Andy and me off a few blocks away from the Pilgrim House Inn. Rolling our luggage onto Spring Street, we passed by the H.P. Lovecraft-style Trinity Church and admired how the moonlight reflected off the church's classic spire, built in 1726.

As we rolled into the historic Pilgrim House Inn, we were greeted by leftover Halloween decorations on the porch of the 1775-era home. We were the only guests slotted to stay in the bed and breakfast that crisp autumn evening. Believe it or not, I had little-to-no knowledge of the Pilgrim House Inn's ghostly past. Unbeknownst to me, we were put into one of the inn's most haunted rooms on the second floor, which is believed to be frequented by a ghost girl nicknamed Jessica.

We cautiously unpacked our luggage in Room 8. On the wall next to my bed were two creepy Victorian-era paintings of what looked like not-so-happy children. There was also a stuffed bunny rabbit on my bed, which oddly served as a trigger object for the inn's ghost girl.

Pilgrim House Inn in Newport, Rhode Island boasts Victorian-style rooms decorated with antique furnishings, and it is reportedly home to a ghost girl. *Photo by Sam Baltrusis.*

For the record, innkeeper Debbie Fonseca started collecting rabbit keepsakes as a kid, and the collection quickly multiplied until stuffed bunnies now occupy nearly every corner of the inn. We were surrounded by bunnies ... and ghosts.

"In the haunted room at the Pilgrim House Inn in Newport," I reported on social media. "I heard a mysterious sobbing of what sounded like a little girl at exactly 2 a.m., which immediately followed the muted chimes of the Trinity Church bell, which was literally around the corner. It was such a beautiful and creepy experience."

Of course, my tone changed once I was able to uncover some of the Pilgrim House Inn's haunted history.

When the British ransacked Newport during the Revolutionary War, most of the city's historic homes were destroyed and used as firewood. In fact, nearly 800 homes were decimated. Oddly, the row of houses on Historic Hill next to Trinity Church were untouched.

"The Pilgrim House Inn building reflects, in its own history, the history of Newport," reported the website *HauntedHouses.com*. "As the economy in Newport began to take off for the first time, in the years before the Revolutionary War, people had flocked to Newport, and new, lovely homes were built, right in the Historic Hill District. The Pilgrim House Inn structure was first built to be a private residence for the new upper-class, probably a merchant's family."

After the British fled, Newport was besieged by deadly epidemics exacerbated by sewage contamination, and the town's children and elderly died from cholera and typhoid during the early nineteenth century.

"The Pilgrim Inn structure was the home of an Irish family, sometime in the 1800s, and they probably lived on the third floor," continued *HauntedHouses.com*. "The Currens, who had three children, left behind a letter they had meant to send to a relative in Ireland, describing their family; children James, Margaret and perhaps a baby Jessica."

The Pilgrim House Inn's resident ghost earned the nickname Jessica after a cleaning lady had a close encounter with a young female spirit. The structure had a past life as a homeless shelter for men, a private residence and eventually an inn.

"She loves to ring the intercom buzzer in empty rooms. For reasons we don't understand, Jessica prefers rooms 8 and 11," wrote John T. Brennan in *Ghosts of Newport*. "In those rooms guests report seeing unexplained shadowy movements and hearing the laughter of a little child."

According to Brennan, one guest left an ominous note in the inn's log confirming the rumors that Room 8 is the inn's most paranormally active. "I don't know if you'll believe me, but this room is haunted. Perhaps she is looking for someone she knows." Also, one couple claimed to have heard "what sounded like a music box coming from the next room."

The *Ghosts of Newport* author said the young female spirit has been spotted by ghost tour groups standing outside of the historic Spring Street structure. "One tour group has reported to have spotted a ghost of Jessica standing in the doorway on a hot summer night," wrote Brennan. "A little girl in an old-fashioned gray dress appeared at the bottom of the stairs and then vanished. A quick check with hotel staff confirmed there were no children staying in the inn."

After a sleepless night at the Pilgrim House Inn, we visited the beautiful Newport mansions. At The Breakers, I felt a strong presence of the Vanderbilt matriarch, Alice, in her bedroom. For dinner, we ate at one of the oldest taverns in the country, the White Horse, dating back to the 1600s. Is it haunted? Absolutely. The paranormal activity is upstairs next to the men's bathroom. I purposely didn't read about the White Horse Tavern's haunted history because I like to use my intuition to guide me. I was right. Upstairs is where the lodging was during the Revolutionary War era, and this is where the man wearing Colonial-era garb has been spotted. My "ghostdar" led me near the fireplace, which is supposedly where a man died while downing a few ales and was found slouched over a table.

Did I see his ghost? No. Was his psychic imprint still there? Yes.

After our evening of spirited dining, we headed back to the haunted Pilgrim House Inn. Our second night was less eventful at the inn except for what sounded like a mysterious scratching at our window. The following morning, I asked the innkeepers about the phantom crying I heard the night before. "That's weird," mused Barry Fonseca, Debbie's husband. He reconfirmed that we were the only guests staying at the inn. "She's usually laughing," he said with an eerie grin.

After taking in the breathtaking views from the inn's third-floor deck, I quickly packed my bags and said a little prayer for the ghost girl known as Jessica.

Chapter 8

BLACK SWAN INN
TILTON, NEW HAMPSHIRE
MOST HAUNTED: #8

.

"I'm sure there are guests who have stayed here and are afraid to say anything. But we often have people who ask, 'don't you know that you have spirits here?' and we usually nod back."

—*Patricia Basiliere, co-owner of the Black Swan Inn*

My psychic bestie Kristene Gulla and I took a wrong turn heading to an overnight investigation at the Black Swan Inn in Tilton, New Hampshire. We jokingly called the dead-end street "Hatchet Lane" because we both picked up on major Native American energy in the area.

After a bizarre roundabout, we ended up at our final destination located next to Tilton's picturesque Winnipesaukee River. As far as the structure's hauntings are concerned, Gulla and I were both contacted before the overnight investigation by a female spirit we later identified as "Belle," the daughter of the 1880s-era building's previous owner. She was waiting for us.

The Black Swan Inn began as the manor of Tilton Tweed manufacturer Selwin Peabody in the late 1800s and was later the home of Arthur S. Brown, whose Tilton Endless Belts were used in the Model T automobile. "Selwin Peabody's daughter Isabella inherited the house and the mill at about eighteen years old. She married a telegraph operator at the town's railroad with the name Arthur Brown," explained John Basiliere, who co-owns the Black Swan Inn with his wife, Patricia.

"Brown ran the mill for a little bit, but he wound up inventing the endless belt, the fan belt on older cars. He was friends with Ford, Firestone and Edison. Ford visited here and wanted to buy his factory. Brown turned him down. Arthur Brown passed away about 1959, and his estate sold the house to Dr. Frank Robinson who practiced here from 1959 to 1982," continued the innkeeper.

Multiple ghosts haunt the Black Swan Inn, a boo-tique hotel in Tilton, New Hampshire, including the inn's former owners. *Photo by Jason Baker.*

The doctor's wife sold the house in 1986 to a couple known as the Fosters, and they turned it into a bed and breakfast. It's been an inn for more than three decades, and John and Patricia "Trish" Basiliere continued the tradition when they purchased the historic property in 2013. The couple said the inn's ghosts called to them … literally.

"John and I are paranormal investigators so that is what interested us in the inn from the beginning," explained Patricia. "There are definitely people who have experienced activity here."

Basiliere said her first paranormal experience at the Black Swan Inn happened when she visited on Halloween in 2012. "My husband and I decided to dress up in period Victorian clothing. Two older ladies arrived a bit early and were in the dining room. I heard my name 'Trish' said very loud and very clear," explained Basiliere. "I thought it was my husband, and, to be honest, I was a little annoyed. I put the book down and headed to the kitchen to ask my husband why he just called my name. He said that he didn't. We have had a very direct communication with the spirits here and at the time were just helping the previous owners."

According to the innkeepers, guests of the Black Swan Inn have encountered the ghosts of the original owners, including Selwin Peabody, Arthur Brown and his wife Isabella, known as "Belle."

"There are definitely people who have experienced activity here. One guy said he felt someone jumping in bed next to him, but there was nobody there. He was very freaked out. One person felt the bed shake in the Belle Room," she said. "There are times that we are here alone, and we'll hear a door close, or inexplicable things will happen."

Basiliere continued, "We hear about paranormal activity in the inn all the time, from people being touched or people hearing voices as if a conversation is going on but they can't hear what's being said … and they will be the only ones in the inn. I'm sure there are guests who have stayed here and are afraid to say anything. But we often have people who ask, 'don't you know that you have spirits here?' and we usually nod back."

Several guests who were with me on the night of the 555 Paranormal Productions investigation said they believed the basement area is extremely active. Residual energy has been psychically imprinted by Dr. Robinson, who used the space as his office.

Sylvia Bean, who participated in the investigation, grew up in New Hampshire's Lakes Region. She said Tilton's doctor had an old-school approach to medicine that may have carried over into the afterlife. "He had no respect for women and young girls who got pregnant," Bean recalled. "I was pregnant when I was fifteen, and he wasn't very nice. There were not a lot of doctors here, and people went to him for everything."

Brandie Wells, a psychic medium who organized the Black Swan investigation, psychically connected with the cellar dweller. "I was in the basement a few years ago, and I didn't know it was a doctor's office at the time," Wells said. "I connected with a doctor, and he was a very dominant, overbearing energy. There's also a teen boy I connect with in the basement. I don't know if that was one of his patients?"

One of the investigators, Robbie Robbins, captured an EVP, or electronic voice phenomenon, in the basement when he asked if "Doc Robinson" was in the house. The disembodied voice said, "I'm present."

In addition to the paranormally active cellar, the Black Swan Inn's owners said the second floor seems to be the historic building's most haunted location. "Most recently, we have a room on the third floor, and it's right above a location that has reported activity," explained Trish. "At 4 a.m., I heard a male clearing his voice, and I knew it wasn't John. Then I heard very clearly, 'Bill, I'm in the hallway.' It sounded like it was coming from the room with the massage table, and John woke up. I was like, 'John, there is somebody in the room below.' I asked the couple staying below if they heard anything weird, and the wife said her husband slept like a rock. So we have no idea who or what that was."

During our investigation at the Black Swan Inn, Gulla and I had a close encounter with "Belle" on the second floor next to what is believed to be an enchanted mirror. In fact, Gulla channeled the woman's spirit during an impromptu séance with our group, which included Jennifer Morrill. During the face-to-face encounter with the ghost, my FLIR thermal camera picked up what looked like an outline of a full-bodied apparition. Morrill and her friends heard what sounded like a mysterious crackling noise while the lights turned on and off.

At one point during the investigation, a lamp on the third floor started to shake inexplicably. Patricia, the co-owner, said it's common for heavy objects throughout the Black Swan Inn to move mysteriously. "Sometimes we will be lying in bed, and our bed will start to shake. The first time it happened, we thought it was an earthquake," she said. "This house was built on granite. The last time it happened, it started with the TV, and then the TV stand and then our bed started to shake. John asked the spirit if they could make it stop, and it stopped. My husband and I are paranormal investigators so John asked if the spirit could do it again, and sure enough it started up again."

Brandie Wells, a psychic-medium who organized the overnight 555 Paranormal Productions investigation, has hosted three events at the Black Swan Inn and is "familiar with the various ghosts on the property," she said, adding that the ghosts of Brown and his wife Belle are still lingering in the inn. "Mr. Brown was a stout man who enjoyed an occasional cigar in his library, and many have reported smelling his cigar," Wells explained. "As a psychic medium, my first encounter was in the library where he presented himself sitting in a chair holding a history book and smoking his cigar."

Wells, who was scratched by a wayward spirit during the investigation I attended, said Brown's wife Isabella still wanders the inn's labyrinthine halls. "Belle has been witnessed as an apparition in her room on the second floor. She also likes to move objects throughout the house. On occasion, you can hear a piano playing in the parlor, and it is said that Belle enjoyed piano."

The mirror, which was right next to the room I stayed in at the inn, is believed to be enchanted. "The mirror at the top of the master staircase is believed to be a portal by many," Wells added.

Photographer Jason Baker and I spent the night in the Selwin Peabody Room, which is believed to be one of the inn's most haunted rooms. According to investigation attendee Sylvia Bean, "If you leave yourself open to it, you will get the best night's sleep ever."

How did I sleep? Believe it or not—I was out like a light.

Chapter 9

PROVINCETOWN INN
PROVINCETOWN, MASSACHUSETTS
MOST HAUNTED: #9

"I believe Provincetown has tons of spirits. People were building empires, and the more energy that surrounds that kind of situation, the more likely there will be spirits lingering about."

—*Adam Berry, TLC's "Kindred Spirits"*

It's no surprise I was put into the one room at the Provincetown Inn that's allegedly haunted. I've stayed in this *The Shining*-esque hotel with its killer views of the harbor many times since I moved back to Boston in 2007. I never scored the so-called haunted room, which is No. 23, until Halloween night a few years ago.

It was after midnight, and, of course, I couldn't sleep a wink.

The wing I was staying in is usually off limits—unless the place is at max capacity, or it's winter. My room was facing the harbor, and I spent most of the evening transfixed by the view of the Pilgrim Monument and the water.

Unfortunately, I had no ghostly encounters at the Provincetown Inn that night in 2015. However, I have seen what appeared to be an inexplicable shadow glide down the hallway one New Year's Eve night a few years ago.

When the team from the Provincetown ParaCon was on the hunt for a host hotel in May 2017, I immediately suggested the allegedly haunted Provincetown Inn. The three-day event was a huge success, and I assembled a motley crew of paranormal A-listers, including Provincetown's own Adam Berry from TLC's *Kindred Spirits, Ghost Hunters* and *Ghost Hunters Academy*. At the paranormal convention, Berry accompanied Amy Bruni, his fellow investigator from *Ghost Hunters* and on-air partner from *Kindred Spirits*.

We held Saturday's main event in the hotel's Harborview Room. I had no idea it had a past life as a disco in the 1970s and a mafia hangout during the 1940s and '50s. Eric Anderson, the group sales manager at the inn, told me he'd heard several reports of shadow figures darting past the storage area. "If we did have a haunted area in the hotel, it would be here," Anderson said, pointing to a room holding furniture and other anachronisms from the 1980s. "There was a disco in that room and all sorts of things happened here."

Known as the spot where the Pilgrims first set foot on Cape Cod in 1620, it's no surprise that Provincetown, Massachusetts is a hotspot for both tourists and hauntings. *Photo by Sam Baltrusis.*

During our "true crime investigation" with Rachel Hoffman and psychic-medium Lucky Belcamino from PXP 2.0, we did pick up some strange light and temperature anomalies in the former disco. After a spirited discussion with a long-time Provincetown resident who was friends with the town's notorious serial killer, Tony "Chop Chop" Costa, we headed outside and had a close encounter with a possible hitchhiker ghost near the park commemorating the place where the Pilgrims first landed in Provincetown on November 11, 1620.

Jeffrey Doucette, co-founder of the former Haunted Ptown ghost tour, said the Outer Cape's most haunted locations have been turned into cozy bed-and-breakfast hideaways. "Provincetown is an old fishing community," he explained. "And when there's an old building with a weird historical backstory, there's potential for it to be haunted."

Over the years, Doucette has spent a lot of time crashing at the Provincetown Inn. Built in 1925, the West End haunt looks creepy. But Doucette isn't convinced it's haunted. "Every time I stay at the Ptown Inn, I expect the two girls from *The Shining* to show up," he mused. "But I haven't had a 'redrum' experience there yet."

However, he does think Ptown boasts a higher-than-usual percentage of haunted guest houses. Why? Doucette, who is a veteran tour guide in Boston, said there's a distinct difference between the haunted hotels near the Boston Common, like the Omni Parker House, and the overnight dwellings scattered throughout Provincetown. "What's interesting about Ptown is that a lot of the active old homes have been turned into guest houses. They weren't hotels or bed and breakfasts to begin with ... they were homes," he said. "Provincetown's haunted corridor is Johnson Street with the Carpe Diem, Christopher's By The Bay and a slew of others around the corner."

The tour guide, who works in the finance department at a publishing house in Government Center when he's not moonlighting as a tour guide, said he was raised in a superstitious Irish Catholic family. "My grandmother was a tinker, or an Irish gypsy, and she would go to confession, and then she would read Tarot cards to make sure she was covering both ends of the spectrum," he joked. "I suspect a little of that tinker mysticism was passed on to me. My mother would always say people would die in threes. When someone passed, we made sure we left the windows open to let the spirits out."

Doucette was an amused skeptic until he gave his first Boston tour in 2009. "A kid on the tour shot a photo of me, and there were all of these white orbs near the Great Elm site," he explained. "The last photo really threw me for a loop. It was of me with a green light coming out of my belly, and I was freaked out." The tour guide said he reached out to a psychic who told him that the green light emanating from his torso was an indication that the spirits in the Boston Common liked the way he told their stories. "At the hanging elm, many of the people who were hanged there were done so unjustifiably by the puritans for crimes they didn't commit. If anyone disagreed with the status quo at that time, they were executed.

Boston was founded by puritans, and it was either their way or the highway ... or the hangman's noose."

Provincetown, in comparison, was where those who challenged the status quo would go to escape the puritanical oppressors. Doucette said having launched the now-defunct Haunted Ptown tour has given him a completely different perspective on the Outer Cape vacation spot. "What I've learned from the tour is that Provincetown is more than a gay tourist destination," he continued. "You have 400 years of history with a vibrant maritime past. So much has happened on this tiny strip of land. Of course it's haunted."

Any surprises from the Provincetown tour? "There are gay ghosts," he said. "It's an LGBT enclave, so it's to be expected. In other cities you don't have a ghost like Preston at the Rose & Crown. He was a drag queen and likes to make himself known during Carnival Week," Doucette explained. "If some drunk queen throws his wig on the ground, he's going to pick it up. Many spirits repeat behaviors that they did when they were alive. He was known to be a caretaker, and it has continued into the afterlife."

So, what inn creeps out Doucette the most? "Carpe Diem, without a doubt," he shot back. "I wouldn't be caught dead there."

The literary-themed bed and breakfast known as Carpe Diem, located at 12 Johnson St. in Provincetown, had a past life as Provincetown's funeral home.

Dead poet's society? Yep, the inn is notoriously haunted. In fact, the William Shakespeare suite, Room 9, is where guests sense an otherworldly presence, as if someone or something is standing behind them. In the Eugene O'Neill suite, workers have seen an imprint of a body on the bed when no one was in the room. There have also been reports of disembodied voices and shadow figures in the basement and a female apparition sporting black, turn-of-the-century clothing walking down the stairs. It's no surprise that bodies were kept in the lower level, awaiting the embalming process and burial, in what was Provincetown's only funeral parlor.

One of the ghosts believed to haunt the inn is a former house manager who loved the property so much he decided to stick around. Seize the day? Apparently, the Latin phrase is applicable even after they're six feet under.

Two former employees, who wish to remain anonymous, told me that the two-story, three-bay building is indeed active. "My first day on the job, I heard footsteps coming up from downstairs and then a door slam," reported a former housekeeper. "I had no idea it was a funeral parlor. I asked, 'is this place haunted?' and I was told that it was."

Jeffrey Doucette, tour guide with Haunted Ptown, said the Carpe Diem's ghost has a name. "Kevin is still there," Doucette confirmed. "Kevin was a manager, and he apparently had a room downstairs. They called him the cellar dweller. He worked there for a long time. Anytime they're downstairs, people report cold spots and footsteps going up the stairs. When they hear the phantom footsteps, they say it's Kevin."

Doucette said bodies were kept on ice in the carriage house at what is now the Carpe Diem. The structure, built in 1870, had a past life as the Trade Winds Inn. It's believed that Kevin managed the property during the pre-Carpe Diem era.

Mark Jasper, author of *Haunted Cape Cod*, interviewed the owners when the structure was newly renovated. He said a housekeeper reported a presence "as if someone was watching him or standing behind him."

Jasper also confirmed the ghostly shenanigans in the basement. "The same housekeeper mentioned that while in the basement, he once heard someone talking in his ear and could actually feel someone's breath on the back of his neck. But when he turned around, he could find no one." Another housekeeper reported seeing a mysterious figure walking into the room in the basement.

Jasper wrote about the rumors surrounding the Carpe Diem's cellar dweller, Kevin. "One of the ghosts is believed to be a former manager named Kevin who died years ago," wrote Jasper. "Apparently, he loved the inn so much his spirit is thought to have remained, looking after things. The identities of the other ghosts remain uncertain."

According to recent reports, activity at the house was exacerbated when the inn was under construction. "Paranormal activity seems to fluctuate at the Carpe Diem," continued Jasper. "At times, the guest house will become extremely active and then for unknown reasons, things will quiet down."

Perhaps Kevin is taking a post-mortem vacation away from the inn he loved to death?

What makes Provincetown's paranormally active inns unique? Compared to larger metropolitan areas replete with haunted hotels and spooktacular bed and breakfast spots, Ptown's overnight haunts are typically former homes.

In fact, many of the spirits allegedly lingering in the Outer Cape might be a byproduct of the strong-willed New England desire to maintain the old buildings of the past, which act as lures to both visitors and ghosts. "Spirits are attracted to the places they lived in," opined the late Jim McCabe, who was a noted ghost-lore expert. "I think what attracts ghosts up here is that you don't tear down the buildings."

Crowne Pointe Historic Inn, located at 182 Bradford St., is a 140-year-old restored estate that stands as an eerie sentinel on a hill. It has forty rooms and a resident, salty-dog spirit. The owners believe that a sea captain who used to own the place haunts their establishment.

Of course, Crowne Pointe Inn isn't the only haunted inn on the block with alleged paranormal activity.

Christopher's By The Bay, located on Johnson Street, was built in 1843 for ship caulker Stephen Mott and his wife Eveline. The Victorian bed and breakfast boasts a female presence on the second floor. Two children are also reported to haunt the house, and patrons in the guest rooms claim that books mysteriously fly off the shelves.

At the Atlantic Light Inn, formerly called the Black Pearl Inn, located at 11 Pearl St., it's said that at least two of the rooms in the 1830s-era inn are haunted.

Animals refuse to enter Room 6, and a full-bodied apparition and inexplicable bloodstains have been seen in Room 7. Zeke Cabal, who was known for his drunken shenanigans in the 1920s, is rumored to haunt the building and hide behind the corner desk in the inn's living room.

At the ShireMax Inn, located at 5 Tremont St. in the West End, guests have reported hearing phantom footsteps. They are believed to be those of a Vietnam War veteran of Portuguese descent who committed suicide by hanging himself in the building because of a broken heart. According to lore, he fell in love with an African-American woman and his family disapproved. Guests report hearing footsteps going down the stairs and the sound of the front door slamming when no one is around.

My first face-to-face haunted encounter in Provincetown was at Revere Guest House on Court Street. Staying in Room 8 on the top level, I watched in awe as the doorknob turned, and I saw what looked like a nineteenth-century fisherman pass through the small hallway from neighboring Room 7. During a second visit, I heard what sounded like a single marble roll down the hall.

According to the former owner, Gary Palochko, a sea captain named Jackson Rogers from the Azores owned the house in the 1860s, and, during renovations in 2004, the B&B owner uncovered a nineteenth-century map. When I mentioned my spirited encounter, Palochko shrugged and said ghosts "scare customers away." However, he said that inexplicable noises heard by previous guests in Room 8 stopped once he found the map and other hidden treasures from the 1860s.

Based on historical research, the fisherman Rogers lived in the house with his wife Mary and their three children, Jennie, Manuel and Joseph. Based on my experience and other reports, the paranormal activity sounded like a residual haunting or a non-intelligent, videotaped replay of past events.

What about the weird sound I heard in the hall? The Revere Guest House owner sheepishly told me that he also uncovered an antique marble buried within the walls.

Crowne Pointe Inn got a makeover in 1999, and the new owners made a concerted effort to return the five-building structure, including the main house owned by the salty sea captain, to its original nineteenth-century glory. "The stately mansion that is now the main house of the Crowne Pointe Historic Inn was built near the turn of the nineteenth century for a prosperous sea captain of the Provincetown Harbor," the inn's website reported. "The grand carriage houses that stand behind the main residence, which housed numerous fishermen once upon a time, were constructed shortly after."

Apparently, the sea captain liked how his former home was restored and continues to make a post-mortem return to his stately abode.

"A very old man believed to be the original inn's sea captain is seen pacing the hallways of the main inn," continued the website. "A ghostly image, often spotted on lobby surveillance cameras, shows a person wearing a flowing white robe, briskly strolling through the lobby late at night. A heavy kitchen door mysteriously opens in the evening and then closes again without human assistance."

Paranormal experts compare the ghosts at Crowne Pointe Inn to Boston's Omni Parker House. Why? Both hotels are supposedly haunted by their former owners.

Arguably the most haunted hotel in New England since opening its doors in October 1855, the Omni Parker House has been home to various sightings of the apparition of the hotel's founder, Harvey Parker, who reportedly has been spotted roaming the tenth-floor annex, checking up on unsuspecting guests. Other spooky happenings involve elevators mysteriously being called to the third floor—once frequented by both Charles Dickens and Henry Wadsworth Longfellow. That's also where the gender-bending lesbian actress, Charlotte Cushman, and an unnamed businessman died. In fact, one third-floor guest room—yes, the mythic Room 303—was supposedly converted into a closet after the unexplained reports of raucous laughter and the smell of whiskey spooked the management.

Like the marketing team at the Omni Parker House, staff at Crowne Pointe Inn have embraced the hotel's alleged ghostly inhabitants. In fact, Crowne Pointe Inn has posted a page on its website dedicated to ghost lore about an old-man specter keeping watch on his old home in the wee hours of the night. "Generations of guests and staff have regularly experienced events that would cause even the staunchest skeptic to take pause," the site mused. "Don't worry, all of our 'extra' visitors are friendly—so far."

Provincetown-based Berry said it's common for a historic structure's original owner to stick around in the afterlife. "My theory is that when one person works so hard to build an empire, whether it's a city, a business or [Crowne Pointe Inn], they can still be around trying to check on what's going on and how those still there are running the place," said Berry. "I believe Provincetown has tons of spirits. People were building empires, and the more energy that surrounds that kind of situation, the more likely there will be spirits lingering about."

Chapter 10

SALEM INN

SALEM, MASSACHUSETTS
MOST HAUNTED: #10

"We are hearing noises all over the place—footsteps, a baby crying, a scratching noise. There are bangs coming from the basement. So many things."

—*Diary entry from overnight guest at the Salem Inn*

An inexplicable supernatural energy emanates from the high-ceilinged Victorian rooms in the Salem Inn. Besides being one of the cozier accommodations in Salem, it's also allegedly one of its most haunted. Reports of disembodied voices, doors mysteriously opening and closing, shadow figures and phantom footsteps have been chronicled in a diary kept in the lobby's sitting room. Guests can enjoy a complimentary glass of sherry and a creepy ghost story or two at this historic hotspot.

Comprised of three homes, the Captain West House is by far its largest and arguably most active. The Federal-style mansion's namesake, Captain Nathaniel West, was married to Elizabeth Derby. The couple seemed to have it all, including money and prestige. But apparently not marital bliss. They divorced in the early 1800s after a highly publicized legal brawl. At the trial, dozens of prostitutes living in the area gathered to testify against West. Ex-wife Derby passed away in 1814, and West remarried in the mid-1830s. The wealthy sea captain's brick mansion was built in 1834 on the land formerly owned by witch trials judge Jonathan Corwin.

As far as hauntings are concerned, West is believed to haunt the upper floors. The full-bodied apparition of a middle-aged woman has been spotted in the building's creepy basement breakfast room. Apparently, she likes to peek into the courtyard from a window.

A child spirit has also been reported. "The staff has tales of a prankster child ghost that runs up and down the staircase and along the upstairs hallways. Doors will open and slam. Small pebbles will be tossed at the clerks working the lobby desk. Guests report items in their rooms being moved about and discovered in a new location," reported *Haunted Places Examiner* website.

Reports of disembodied voices, doors mysteriously opening and closing, shadow figures and phantom footsteps have been chronicled in a diary kept in the Salem Inn's sitting room. The Salem Inn's house spirit Catherine is believed to inhabit Room 17. *Photo by Sam Baltrusis.*

However, Room 17 seems to be the most active. Based on reports kept in the diary, guests have experienced a "filmy white apparition" of a woman sitting on their bed in the Jacuzzi room. People in the same house have been kept awake by loud pounding and banging noises on the walls and ceilings throughout the night. Phantom gunshots have also been heard in Room 17.

"My husband was in the shower and I was in bed with my eyes closed," reported one woman in the diary. "I felt someone sit on the edge of the bed beside me. Thinking it was my husband, I opened my eyes to say something—but he was still in the bathroom. It felt more like a child's weight than an adult weight."

Another guest reported seeing a "dark figure in a long coat and rain hat." She asked him who he was, and the spirit of Room 17 responded cryptically, "Don't touch me, the dullness rubs off."

It's believed that the female apparition in the room is called Catherine. "She is often recognized as a sudden cool breeze that whisks past visitors on the stairs or hallways," continued the *Haunted Places Examiner*. "Or perhaps she is the disembodied voice one hears on a quiet night chatting to a gentleman about their child. She has been sighted in and around Room 17. Ghost hunters have recorded voices when using a ghost box."

Other guests report the phenomenon known as sleep paralysis—the feeling of "being pinned down and frozen in bed"—in Room 13. Others have seen their doorknob turn, as if someone is trying to enter the room, but no one's there. One family was creeped out by inexplicable noises: "We are hearing noises all over the place—footsteps, a baby crying, a scratching noise. There are bangs coming from the basement. So many things."

Disembodied voices and shadow figures are common in Room 40. "I woke up about dawn and saw a figure standing on the balcony," reported one guest. "I sat up quickly and said, 'Who are you?' The figure was suddenly gone."

Of course, the owner of the Salem Inn believes the ghost lore is nonsense. "Please note that we have many guests who write about their visitations and experiences with the supernatural or hauntings or whatever," wrote Diane Pabich. "Neither we, the owners, nor any of the staff have had such occurrences. I personally think it is the power of suggestion and the fact that these guests are visiting Salem with its fascinating history."

However, employees swear the common sensation of a cold breeze whooshing by them in the lobby is the Salem Inn's house spirit Catherine.

Chapter 11

THE KENNEBUNK INN
KENNEBUNK, MAINE
MOST HAUNTED: #11

"It felt like someone came right up next to me, and I heard a voice say, 'Muuuah.' It was definitely a loud moan. Whoever did it was obviously trying to test me—to see whether I'd run or stay. It was somebody who was menacing. He had a menacing side to him."
—Diane de Seversky, The Kennebunk Inn

It was a dark-and-stormy train ride to Southern Maine. Seriously. It reminded me of a scene from a Stephen King novel or the opening sequence to the TV show *Dark Shadows*. On a whim, I hopped on the Downeaster Amtrak leaving from Boston's North Station over Labor Day weekend. I literally let the ghosts guide me to this rustic Maine hotspot after pulling The Kennebunk Inn from a hat chock-full of potential haunted hotels. I had no idea that the ghost of the famous poet, Silas H. Perkins, would literally greet me when I walked into the historic Kennebunk Inn.

Built as the private home of Phineas Cole, the structure served as a family residence for an obstetrician, Dr. Frank Ross, before a man called George Baitler converted it into a hotel known as "The Tavern." He added an additional wing with two floors and recrafted the building to accommodate fifty rooms. Renamed The Kennebunk Inn in the 1930s, the hotel fell into disrepair and was purchased and refurbished by Arthur and Angela LeBlanc in 1978. It was during the renovations that reports of paranormal activity started to surface.

I didn't know much about the 1799-era structure's haunted reputation before trekking up the coast. For years, the inn's resident spirit was nicknamed Cyrus. "Many have claimed that they could sense his presence, while others have actually stated that they have seen him as if he was still performing his work," reported the website *HauntedPlacesToGo.com*. "Then, there are the cases where glasses for wine and other objects have suddenly moved on their own, fallen and even seemed to have been thrown in various areas as if the man is attempting to gain the attention of the living."

Two spirits with similar names—Silas and Cyrus—haunt Maine's the Kennebunk Inn. *Photo by Sam Baltrusis.*

According to Thomas D'Agostino's *Legends, Lore and Secrets of New England,* the inn's former employee Pattie Farnsworth had a close encounter with a male spirit during the 1980s while carrying provisions to the storage area in the restaurant's cellar. The name "Cyrus" immediately popped up in Farnsworth's mind after the face-to-face experience, and her nickname for the persnickety phantom circulated for years.

Staff at the first-floor restaurant have reported all sorts of ghostly shenanigans, including glasses levitating, place settings inexplicably moving and doors opening and closing without an explanation. A former bartender claimed that a spirit assaulted him with a beer mug one night. "The force with which the bartender was hit left a bump on his head," wrote Roxie Zwicker in *Haunted York County.* "He felt that the mug had been deliberately thrown at him."

The activity seemed to intensify when the structure was renovated. The employees and owners blamed the potential poltergeist activity on Cyrus.

It wasn't until a family member of the late, great poet, Silas Perkins, visited the inn to reminisce about the writer's last few years working at The Kennebunk Inn as a night auditor in the 1950s when the staff started to put the pieces together.

Was the house ghost Silas Perkins?

"In June 1952, seventy-two-year-old Silas Perkins strolled out of the inn to buy a newspaper. His heart gave out, and he was carried back to the inn," wrote D'Agostino, adding that he died on the second floor. "His permanent status at the inn still seems to continue, as Mr. Perkins refuses to give up his position as part of the staff."

The room Perkins actually died in is up for debate. D'Agostino said it was the fireplace room, which is Room 11. In multiple newspaper accounts, the inn's most haunted location is Room 17, where the current owners, acclaimed chefs Shanna and Brian O'Hea, believed the poet passed away.

Is it Silas or Cyrus? Both. O'Hea said The Kennebunk Inn is home to more than one spirit. According to an article in the *Bangor Daily News* from October 2014, both a Silas and a Cyrus haunt the inn. Apparently, the more aggressive Cyrus once worked the front desk. There's also a little girl named Emily. The owner told reporter Seth Koenig that the child spirit is "playful, running up and down the hallways and knocking on the doors."

A former front-desk employee, Diane de Seversky, told Koenig: "It felt like someone came right up next to me, and I heard a voice say, 'Muuuah.' It was definitely a loud moan. Whoever did it was obviously trying to test me—to see whether I'd run or stay. It was somebody who was menacing. He had a menacing side to him."

As for my ghostly experiences at The Kennebunk Inn, I encountered more than one spirit during a recent overnight stay. I recorded my experiences online and several psychic-mediums claimed that a balding man followed me all over the house. A male energy with a thin stature and a child spirit also made themselves felt. In my room on the second floor, I picked up two words on the Ovilus, "poem" and "read."

George Baitler converted the haunted structure located at 45 Main St. into "The Tavern" in 1928, and the watering hole eventually became The Kennebunk Inn in the late 1930s. *Photo courtesy of the Boston Public Library, Print Department.*

Perkins—whose poem "The Common Road" was syndicated nationally from the funeral train of President Franklin Roosevelt—responded when I read his poem out loud. I captured what sounded like footsteps moving closer to me on the wooden floor, which are unusually creaky, followed by a disembodied male voice.

At first, I panicked when I felt the male spirit next me, and then the spirit walked away.

"I just watched your live feed from the haunted hotel," said radio host Solaris BlueRaven. "Most of the heavier energy is downstairs. Your room is very protected. I did notice some kind of energy in your bathroom ceiling area. Enjoy your stay."

After my up-close-and-personal encounter at The Kennebunk Inn, I walked down the street to the Mousam River to ground myself. In the wee hours of the night, the storm had subsided, and the village was a ghost town ... both literally and figuratively. I felt a strong Native American energy next to the Mousam, and, after saying a prayer of protection, I headed back to The Kennebunk Inn for a peaceful night of sleep.

Chapter 12

OMNI PARKER HOUSE
BOSTON, MASSACHUSETTS
MOST HAUNTED: #12

"Our history has many skeletons in its closet, and the spirits want their story to be told. I'm giving a voice to those without a voice."
—Jeffrey Doucette, veteran tour guide

"There are bodies everywhere," I said during a taping of the Biography Channel show *Haunted Encounters: Face To Face* in 2012. "The spot where he had the initial encounter was a mass gravesite."

I was standing in front of Boylston and Tremont, an area I've identified as Boston's haunted corridor thanks to an aura of disaster imprinted by the gas-line explosion of 1897. My face-to-face encounter was with a teen spirit I now call Mary.

While writing my first book *Ghosts of Boston: Haunts of the Hub*, I started spending hours in the Boston Common. I've always felt a strong magnetic pull to the site of the Great Elm, also known as the hanging tree. I had an inexplicable interest in the Central Burying Ground, and one night while walking by the old cemetery, I noticed a young female figure wearing what looked like a hospital gown, standing by a tree. I looked back, and she was gone. At that point, I didn't know about the Matthew Rutger legend dating back to the 1970s. Like me, he saw a ghost at the old cemetery. Somehow, I felt her pain.

A few months after the incident, I joined a group of tour guides who specialize in telling Boston's paranormal history, and it was there that I learned about many of the so-called ghosts from New England's past. While giving tours, including Boston Haunts, I had several encounters with the paranormal at the Omni Parker House.

During my first visit, for example, I heard a disembodied voice whisper "welcome" in my ear. Was it the hotel's founder, Harvey Parker?

While taking a photo in front of the Omni Parker House's "enchanted mirror" on the second-floor mezzanine, author Sam Baltrusis noticed condensation appear on the mirror as if someone, or something, was breathing on it. *Photo by Ryan Miner.*

Over the years, I've stayed away from the hotel, because, from the outside, it had an inexplicably eerie vibe. While taking a photo in front of the famed "enchanted mirror" on the second-floor mezzanine, I noticed condensation mysteriously appear on the mirror, as if someone, or something, was breathing on it. According to hotel lore, the antique was taken from Charles Dickens' room. He apparently stood in front of it to practice his nineteenth-century orations.

As a special treat for guests on my Boston Haunts ghost tour, I would guide them to the supernatural hotspot. While the ghost story is intriguing, what interested me even more is the fact that the press room next to the creepy mirror is where John F. Kennedy announced his candidacy for president. I've seen tons of photos and heard many stories from patrons who had strange encounters while staying on the hotel's upper floors. Today, the Omni Parker House has become one of my favorite haunts in the city. Haunted history oozes from the oldest continuously operating hotel in the country.

Besides being one of the more ornate structures in Boston, the Omni Parker House is also allegedly one of its most haunted. Originally built in October 1855, it boasts a slew of ghostly reports ranging from Harvey Parker himself—who passed away on May 31, 1884, at the age of seventy-nine and apparently continues to roam the halls of the hotel he built—to mysterious orbs floating down the tenth-floor corridor and a malevolent male spirit with a disturbing laugh who reportedly lingers in the recently reopened Room 303.

Parker's rags-to-riches story started in 1826 when he moved to Boston with nothing but a pocketful of change. He saved his nickels and dimes while working as a coachman for a Brahmin socialite and built a restaurant that later became his namesake hotel. Torn down, except for one wing, and rebuilt in its present gilded glory in the late 1920s, the hotel was called the Parker House until the 1990s when the Omni hotel chain purchased the historic structure. The hotel has several claims to fame, including being the birthplace of the Boston cream pie. It's also had a few famous employees, including Ho Chi Minh, who was a busboy, and Malcolm X, who worked as a waiter. John Wilkes Booth stayed at the Parker House eight days before assassinating President Lincoln on April 14, 1865. In fact, he used a shooting gallery not far from the hotel to practice his aim before heading to Ford's Theatre in Washington, D.C.

Other haunted happenings involve elevators mysteriously being called to the third floor—once frequented by both Charles Dickens and Henry Wadsworth Longfellow. The hotel's ornate lifts are known to mysteriously stop on the floor without anyone pushing a button. There's also the story of Room 303, which in 1949 was the scene of a rumored suicide of a liquor salesman who killed himself with barbiturates and whiskey. According to lore, the room is said to have inspired horror legend Stephen King when he wrote the short-story-turned-film "1408."

The Omni Parker House is a stone's throw from the extremely haunted Boston Common.

From its beginnings as a sheep and cow pasture in 1634, just a few years after the city itself was founded, the forty-eight-acre green space purchased from

Boston's first settler, William Blackstone, has since been touted as the oldest city park in the United States. It's also home to some of the darker chapters from Boston's not-so-puritanical past.

The Boston Common is chock-full of ghosts, graves and gallows. It is, in essence, "one big anonymous burying ground," wrote Holly Nadler, author of *Ghosts of Boston Town.* "Under the Puritan regime, untold numbers of miscreants—murderers, thieves, pirates, Indians, deserters, Quakers and putative witches—were executed in the Common" at the so-called Great Elm, which was also nicknamed the hanging tree or gallows tree by locals. "At risk to their own lives, friends and family might sneak in under the cover of darkness, cut down the cadaver and bury it somewhere in the park," continued Nadler. "If no one came forward to deal with the disastrous remains, town officials disposed of them in the river, where bloated bodies frequently washed in and out with the tides."

There was also a mass grave site near the southern corner of the Common, yards away from the designated Central Burying Ground. In early 1895, the human remains of 100 dead bodies were uncovered during the excavation of the nation's first underground trolley station, now the Boylston Green Line stop. A mob scene of "curiosity seekers" lined up along the Boylston Street corner of the Common "looking at the upturning of the soil," according to the April 18, 1895, edition of the *Boston Daily Globe.* The report continued, saying that "a large number of human bones and skulls are being unearthed as the digging on the Boylston Street mall" progressed. Thrill-seeking spectators were horrified by the sights and smells emanating from the site and were forced to move by early May.

And that was just the first round of skeletons in the Common's collective closet. As the excavation continued, officials uncovered the remains of hundreds—some historians estimated between 900 and 1,100 bodies—buried in shallow graves beneath the Boylston mall.

While the nearby Granary Burial Ground earns top billing thanks to its Freedom Trail–friendly names, including Paul Revere, Samuel Adams, John Hancock and even Mother Goose, the Boston Common's lesser-known Central Burying Ground has something that the other graveyards don't: ghosts. After Boston's puritan leaders purchased the plot in 1756, the cemetery was used as a final resting spot for foreigners and other paupers who couldn't cough up enough shillings for a proper burial. The graveyard is the resting spot for composer William Billings and artist Gilbert Stuart, who was responsible for painting George Washington's mug on the dollar bill. It is also reportedly the place where the see-through denizens from the Common's spirit realm prefer to hang out.

"Visitors to the graveyard have reported seeing shadowy figures appear nearby, often near trees," wrote Christopher Forest in *Boston's Haunted History.* "The figures disappear or dissolve when people look right at them. Some people have associated the figures with the former hanging victims who met their end on the Boston Common gallows."

Apparently, the cemetery's spirits like to have fun with tourists. "They have been accused of poking people in the back, rattling keys and even brushing up against shoulders. Some people roaming the graveyard have reported being grabbed from behind by an unseen force," Forest wrote.

Jeffrey Doucette, a veteran tour guide, said he was a skeptic until he witnessed a woman have a close encounter with a paranormal force outside the cemetery's gates in 2011. "She felt someone or something tap her on the shoulder," he mused. "She looked annoyed, and I had to assure her that no one was there."

The more notorious haunting at the Central Burying Ground centers on a young female spirit who was described by the late ghost expert Jim McCabe as a teen girl "with long red hair, sunken cheekbones and a mud-splattered gray dress on." On a rainy afternoon in the 1970s, she paid a visit to a dentist named Dr. Matt Rutger, who reportedly experienced "a total deviation from reality as most of us know it." According to Nadler's *Ghosts of Boston Town*, Rutger was checking out the gravestone carvings. He felt a tap on his shoulder and then a violent yank on his collar. No one was there.

As Rutger was bolting from the cemetery, he noticed something out of the corner of his eye. "I saw a young girl standing motionless in the rear corner of the cemetery, staring at me intently," he said. The mischievous spirit then reappeared near the graveyard's gate, almost fifty yards from the initial encounter. Then the unthinkable happened. "He somehow made it by her to Boylston Street, and even though he couldn't see her, he felt her hand slip inside his coat pocket, take out his keys and dangle them in midair before dropping them," McCabe recounted.

Rutger, in an interview with Nadler, said the '70s-era paranormal encounter had left an indelible mark on his psyche. "One thing is certain, the encounter affected me in very profound ways," he reflected. "As a trained medical professional, I have always seen the world in fairly empirical terms. There's no way something like that cannot completely change how you think about the world."

Based on the freaked-out expression on Haunted Boston tour guide Jeffrey Doucette's face, he looked as if he had just seen a ghost. "You're not going to believe what just happened," he said, rushing into the Omni Parker House's mezzanine watering hole, Parker's Bar, one Sunday evening after giving a ghost tour to a group of high school kids from Vermont. "As I was telling a story at the site of the hanging elm, I could tell something was up," he recalled, packing up his lantern and sitting down at a cozy table near the bar's fireplace. "The chaperone is waving at me as if 'Jeff, you need to look at this,' and she shows me her camera. I literally couldn't believe what I was seeing. In the photo, it looks like seven nooses hanging from the trees in the area near what was the hanging tree."

Doucette, a popular tour guide among out-of-town visitors thanks to his distinct Boston accent, said he was a skeptic for years until he had a few close encounters of the paranormal kind while trudging through the tour's haunted sites scattered throughout the Boston Common and Beacon Hill. Now, he's a full-fledged believer. "I was like, 'What the…? Let's get out of here,'" he said, referring to the noose photo taken earlier in the evening and to creepy pictures of demonic, red-colored orbs shot in the Central Burying Ground. "It literally freaked me out. This year, I've seen a lot of orbs, but nothing like what I just saw. I'm not sure if [the spirits] heard me talking about the interview I'm having with you, but they really showed their colors tonight. The ghosts in the Boston Common were out in full force, and they were screaming."

Doucette was an amused skeptic until he gave his first Boston Common tour in 2009. "A kid on the tour shot a photo of me, and there were all of these white orbs near the Great Elm site," he explained. "The last photo really threw me for a loop. It was of me with a green light coming out of my belly, and I was freaked out. Since then, we've had a few orbs here and there, but this year has been out of control. Tonight, I really don't know what happened. Will I sleep? I don't know. But it was something that I've never experienced before."

The tour guide said he reached out to a psychic who told him that the green light emanating from his torso was an indication that the spirits in the Boston Common liked the way he told their stories. "At the hanging elm, many of the people who were hanged there were done so unjustifiably by the Puritans for crimes they didn't commit. If anyone disagreed with the status quo at that time, they were executed. Boston was founded by Puritans, and it was either their way or the highway ... or the hangman's noose. Even in the modern age, if you disagree with authority, there's the chance that you can be shamed. In my opinion, many of those hanged in the Boston Common were victims of freedom of speech and died at the hands of oppressive authority figures. So when I say on the tour that many of the people hanged at the Great Elm site died innocently, I feel like I'm giving them a voice."

Doucette continued, "I've always been respectful of the spirits in the Boston Common. They've never bothered me at home, and I never had an issue with a haunting. But when I do the tours, they do come out. I've been a strong advocate for those who were disenfranchised and oppressed, especially women, and they always respond to the stories that I tell on the tour."

As far as historical figures are concerned, Doucette said he's drawn to people like Ann "Goody" Glover, who was hanged for allegedly practicing witchcraft on November 16, 1688. Glover, a self-sufficient, strong-willed Irish woman who spoke fluent Gaelic, lived in the North End, where she washed laundry for John Goodwin and his family. After a spirited spat in her native Gaelic tongue with Goodwin's thirteen-year-old daughter, Martha, Glover was accused of bewitching the four children in the household and was sent to prison for practicing the dark arts. While Glover was exonerated of her crimes in 1988 and dubbed a "Catholic martyr" 300 years after her execution, Doucette said he's compelled to tell her story. However, he's not convinced that Glover's spirit is haunting the Boston Common. "People want a big name to associate with the hauntings in the Common, but I seriously don't think that's the case," he said, adding that "it makes for good storytelling."

Doucette, who ends the Haunted Boston ghost tour at the historic Omni Parker House located at 60 School St. near Park Street station, said he's heard many creepy tales while hanging out at Parker's Bar. "I spend a huge amount of time here," he remarked. "There was a night in October, and I came into the bar before a tour. A woman who was in her mid-fifties and working the bar asked if I gave the haunted tour and then told me the creepiest story."

According to the Parker's Bar worker, one guest checked in but had a hard time checking out. There was an early-season snowstorm, and the Parker House guest refused to pay his hotel bill. "As he was leaving and coming out of the School Street entrance, the doormat mysteriously flies up and blocks the exit as he's trying to leave," the tour guide mused. "The guy turns around and pays his bill."

Like Doucette, the man who tried to leave the Parker House without paying his bill was smacked in the face with what could have been a ghost from Boston's past. "Our history has many skeletons in its closet, and the spirits want their story to be told," he said. "I'm giving a voice to those without a voice."

Chapter 13

HAWTHORNE HOTEL
SALEM, MASSACHUSETTS
MOST HAUNTED: #13

"There was so much electricity that night. When we took the haunted elevator to the sixth floor, everybody on the tour said they felt like they were standing on a boat. It felt like waves. We were surrounded by spirit energy in Room 612."
—Colleen F. Costello, psychic medium from TLC's "Paranormal Lockdown"

When it comes to hotels replete with paranormal residue, Salem is a hotbed of paranormal activity. "The Hawthorne Hotel is built on a property that once held a building that burned down six times taking many lives," wrote Christopher Dowgin on *Salem Secret Underground*'s blog. "In its parking lot once stood the Crowninshield-Bentley House, which was featured in H.P. Lovecraft's *Thing on the Doorstep*. Its other parking lot is holy ground for a Jewish Temple that once stood there."

As far as hauntings are concerned, the Hawthorne Hotel allegedly boasts phantom hands in Room 325 and a female, full-bodied apparition on the sixth floor. However, when Syfy's *Ghost Hunters* investigated reports in 2007 of strange sounds like children crying and unseen forces touching guests in the hotel, the crew didn't uncover anything supernatural. Yet enthusiasts continue to claim a female apparition hovers in front of Room 612.

Based on a recent investigation with Amy Bruni's Strange Escapes group, I can say without hesitation that the Hawthorne Hotel's haunted suite on the sixth floor is in fact haunted. Bruni, formerly a long-time investigator on *Ghost Hunters* and currently with TLC's *Kindred Spirits*, asked me to give tours of Salem and the Hawthorne Hotel before her group headed on a cruise ship to Bermuda. I asked my psychic friend Colleen F. Costello, who recently appeared on *Paranormal Lockdown* with Nick Groff and has worked with Bruni in the past, to help me.

"There was so much electricity that night," Costello remembered. "When we took the haunted elevator to the sixth floor, everybody on the tour said they felt like they were standing on a boat. It felt like waves. We were surrounded by spirit energy in Room 612."

Officially opened in 1925, the Hawthorne Hotel is a six-story, 150-room hotel on a piece of land formerly occupied by the fire-prone Franklin Building. *Photo by Sam Baltrusis.*

When Costello and I entered the haunted suite, we both heard a distinct voice demanding that we get out of the room. After that initial encounter, I decided it was in my best interest to spend as little time as possible in the haunted suite. I also invited my friend Rachel Hoffman from Paranormal Xpeditions to help with the investigation while Costello and I gave walking tours throughout Salem. Thankfully, Hoffman led the investigations for the remainder of the night.

Of course, the Hawthorne Hotel isn't the only overnight lodging in Salem known for reports of supernatural activity. The Morning Glory Bed and Breakfast, which is literally across the street from the House of the Seven Gables, has alleged activity in each of the four rooms named after witch trials victims: Elizabeth Howe, Rebecca Nurse, Sarah Good and Bridget Bishop. Psychic mediums who have stayed in the third-floor Sarah Good suite claim to have spotted ghost children jumping up and down on their bed. Supposedly, several children have died in the house, which was built in the early 1800s.

Oddly, psychic Denise Fix, who featured in my book *Ghosts of Cambridge*, talked about a similar experience with kid spirits in her childhood home facing Salem's wharf area. "I was five or six when it first started," she recalled. "I couldn't go to sleep at night, and my mother wanted to know why, and I told her about the kids in my room. She thought it was a nightmare, but I knew it was something else."

Fix said her childhood was like a scene from Stephen King's *It* or *The Shining*. "These kids would appear, and they wanted me to go to a party," she explained. "In my head, I knew if I went to a party with them, I wasn't coming back. And then the ghost kids were like, 'If you don't go to the party, we'll get your sister to go. So, I jumped on my sister to protect her, and she woke up screaming, saying I attacked her. My family thought I was nuts."

In addition to the playful ghost children, the Morning Glory, located at 22 Hardy Street, hosts a teenage girl spirit with long, wavy hair in the Bridget Bishop room. One former guest claimed on the inn's website that the full-bodied apparition of a young woman, between seventeen and twenty years old, manifested in front of her and smiled. "She was dressed in a long gown from the late 1800s, early 1900s," she wrote. "It was white, trimmed in royal or dark blue. She had very light brown or dark blonde hair pulled back off her face, but it cascaded over her shoulders."

Salem's most active? The Hawthorne Hotel continues to make national "haunted hotel" lists even though the team from *Ghost Hunters* didn't capture paranormal activity during its made-for-TV investigation.

Elliott O'Donnell, an Irish author who became an authority on the supernatural during the early 1900s, wrote about a close encounter at a no-name hotel in the area with "an undeniable reputation for being haunted" in his book published in 1917 called *Experiences as a Ghost Hunter.* "I only stayed in town two nights," he wrote, not citing a specific location. "It was in a rather poor neighborhood, and there were few visitors."

O'Donnell, who had an uncanny ability to embroider fact with a grandiose flair for fiction, allegedly chatted with the night porter about the hotel's elevator, which had a mind of its own. "A visitor arrived here late one night and was found by the day porter dead in the lift," the porter recalled. "How he died was never exactly known. It was rumored he had either committed suicide or been murdered ... Since then that elevator has taken into its head to set itself in motion at the same time every night."

Haunted elevators? Yep, it's a recurring theme at a certain Salem hotel where visitors stay a few decades or so beyond checkout time.

History and mystery ooze from the lobby of the Hawthorne Hotel, which opened its gilded doors on July 23, 1925, amid much fanfare and excitement. Approximately 1,110 of the area's residents and businessmen bought stock in what would become the city's grand dame: a six-story, 150-room hotel on a piece of land formerly occupied by the fire-prone Franklin Building.

Yes, the Hawthorne Hotel's site had a history of bad luck, which included a series of destructive fires. "An easterly gale was raging, and the fire progressed, in spite of all of the efforts to save it, until the noble structure, which has been one of our institutions for about sixty years, and which extended from Essex to Forrester street, was a complete mess of ruins," reported the *Salem Register* in the 1800s.

Of course, the building named after Salem's native son Nathaniel Hawthorne has been plagued by less-destructive blazes over the years. In October 1997, a small fire broke out in the hotel's basement and caused an estimated $10,000 in damage. "Smoke reached all six floors of the hotel, and the Hawthorne's main ballroom suffered considerable smoke damage," reported the *Salem Evening News.* Luckily, no one was hurt.

It's possible that the psychic imprint from the cursed land's past may have caused what parapsychologists call an aura of disaster—fertile ground for the birthing of ghosts. According to several accounts over the years, the Hawthorne Hotel does indeed have a storied history of alleged paranormal activity.

"Surrounded by the many grand homes erected by the wealthy sea captains, the Salem Marine Society was founded by the skippers in 1766," wrote Lynda Lee Macken in *Haunted Salem & Beyond.* "The society's building was razed when the town determined it was time to construct the hotel. As a condition of acquiring the land, the hotel's owners agreed to provide a meeting place for the men. Some employees wonder if the spirits of some of those old sea captains have returned."

The Salem Marine Society's secret meeting spot is on the off-limits roof of the Hawthorne Hotel and is an exact replica of a cabin from the *Taria Topan,* one of the last Salem vessels to sail regularly during its golden maritime trips to East India. Several employees and visitors claim that the large ship wheel now in the restaurant mysteriously spins, as if unseen hands are steering it, when no one is there.

Other encounters include water faucets turning on and off and toilets flushing on their own. There have been many reports of disembodied voices echoing throughout the hotel and so-called phantom hands in the structure's allegedly most-active rooms, 325 and 612.

When the TV show *Bewitched* shot several episodes in Salem, the cast and crew used the allegedly haunted Hawthorne Hotel as their home base. In fact, Elizabeth Montgomery's stay in Salem is immortalized in a Samantha Stephens statue in Lappin Park. For those out of the pop-culture loop, Montgomery rode into town to film eight episodes of *Bewitched* during the summer of 1970.

"For years after the two episodes aired as the *Salem Saga*, the hotel desk fielded telephone calls asking if this was the Hawthorne Hotel that was seen on *Bewitched*," reported the hotel's newsletter. In the show, the building was known as the Hawthorne Motor Hotel.

The elevator made famous during its *Bewitched* days apparently has a mind of its own. It's believed to be haunted by an invisible presence, and some say a ghostly woman has taken a ride with them in the elevator. The same female residual haunting has been spotted in rooms and mysteriously disappears when guests confront her.

The Hawthorne Hotel's reputation as Salem's "most haunted" sometimes surpasses its historical significance. In 2007, it made the fourth slot on Travelocity's haunted hotel list, which surveyed overnight haunts across the country.

However, the hotel's general manager said the claims of paranormal activity simply weren't true. In fact, she cited an episode of *Ghost Hunters* shot at the hotel as proof. "There's no documentation," said Juli Lederhaus in the October 24, 2011 report in the *Boston Globe*. "People tell us they feel things, whatever, but we don't have any documentation. Of course, [guests] do look up haunted hotels on the Internet, and those things pop up. The more people cite those kinds of stories, the more they get published out there. I feel like I'm constantly putting out fires."

Oddly, fire may be the "psychic residue" visitors claim to sense when visiting the hotel.

Lederhaus reiterated that the myth—which is perpetuated in several books—that the hotel marks the former site of Bridget Bishop's apple orchard just isn't true. For the record, Bishop's property was near the current spot of the old Lyceum Hall. Investigators with *Ghost Hunters* told the general manager that they had visited the library and City Hall and had conducted research on the physical property and had found that "nothing happened at the hotel that would cause hauntings," she claimed.

Seriously? The TV researchers completely overlooked the six fires that plagued the land's previous occupant, the Franklin Building, during the 1800s. "A few years since, a brick partition wall was erected, and this saved the entire building from destruction and prevented the conflagration from spreading to an untold extent among the wooden structures in the vicinity," reported the *Daily Advertiser* on February 1, 1845.

John Marsicano, a regular visitor to the hotel, said the *Ghost Hunters* investigation shouldn't rule out the possibility of paranormal activity. "I think those guys are good and do their endeavor earnestly and are honest about it," he told the *Globe*. "But ghosts and spirits, if they do anything, might not do it on command."

Of course, Lederhaus did point out that two other buildings existed at the site before the hotel. "Could something have happened in one of those buildings?" she said. "Who knows?"

Sam Baltrusis

THE OTHERS

"I've had the covers ripped off my bed, and I've felt ghostly hands groping my body."
—Joni Mayhan, best-selling author of "Ghost Magnet" and "Bones in the Basement"

Road weary travelers are often in for a surprise when they check into their hotel room for the night. Something doesn't seem right. Strange shadows move in the darkened corners of the room, and mumbled voices fill the silence. They might feel the sensation of being watched and wake up the next morning feeling tired and drained. Sometimes, they experience far worse.

I tend to experience hotels differently than most people. As someone who can feel the presence of ghosts, my experience is usually somewhat terrifying. I am simply not allowed to sleep. Every time I attempt to drift off into a peaceful slumber, something wakes me up. Sometimes it's something fairly harmless, like a light switch turning itself on, but at other times it is far more malevolent.

There have been many times when I've heard footsteps approach my bed and then stop. I lie there with my eyes pressed tightly closed, not wanting to see what's looming over me. As a paranormal investigator, I know I should look because this is often why I'm there, but as a single woman, alone in a room, I seem to forget that. I've had the covers ripped off my bed, and I've felt ghostly hands groping my body. I've never fled a room, but I've come very close several times.

The type of hotel doesn't seem to matter. I've stayed at nice hotels and also the kind you wouldn't want your dog staying in. They're all equally haunted. All it takes is one ghost to make a sensitive's night a living hell.

If you're looking for a spooky evening, spend the night at one of these legendary haunted inns. The ghosts here are interactive and enjoy surprising you with unexpected encounters. In some cases, you might even find yourself with an extra bedmate you weren't counting on.

Recently closed for renovations, The Yankee Pedlar Inn is a historic hotel located in Torrington, Connecticut.

YANKEE PEDLAR INN
TORRINGTON, CONNECTICUT

Currently closed for renovations, the Yankee Pedlar Inn is one of the oldest inns in New England. Built in 1891 by Irish immigrants Frank and Alice Conley, it was originally opened as the Conley Inn. Even though both of the Conleys died in 1910, it's rumored that their ghosts remained behind. Reports of voices and rocking chairs are frequent in Room 353, where Alice supposedly died. People have also witnessed the apparition of Frank appearing in Room 295.

It should come as no surprise that the 41,139-square-foot hotel served as the setting for the 2011 horror movie *The Innkeepers*.

During a recent visit to the inn, I sat in on an Echovox session where the investigators used an instrumental transcommunication device to speak to the dead. They received several clear responses from a woman who told them she died at the hotel years ago.

The ghosts here like to play games of hide-and-seek, appearing just out of the corner of your eye. When you turn to look, they're gone, leaving you wondering what you saw. I experienced this first hand inside the ladies room on the first floor when I witnessed a wispy shape flit past the closed bathroom stall door. It was enough to make me gasp. As a paranormal investigator, this was exactly what I was hoping for.

If you decide to sleep over, be prepared for vivid dreams. You might even find yourself on a tour with the spirit of Frank Conley.

MOST HAUNTED ROOMS: 295 and 353

Located in Durham, New Hampshire, the historic Three Chimneys Inn dates back to 1649.

THREE CHIMNEYS INN
DURHAM, NEW HAMPSHIRE

A filmy white ghost often roams the dark hallways of this haunted inn. While they say she is harmless, she is still a frightening sight in the wee hours of the morning when the inn has settled down for the night.

The ghost also has an affinity for electronics, turning on lights and changing the settings on people's cell phones. She has even mastered the knack of making numbers on a calculator transpose appear backwards on the screen.

One innkeeper had a startling encounter with the roaming ghost. She went to her office after a long day at the inn and discovered that her door was locked. This was strange, because she knew she didn't lock the door, and the only key was in her pocket. She went in and sat down at her computer to check her emails one more time before retiring for the night. When she turned on the screen, a haunting message appeared. "Time to go home and rest," it said. She smiled and turned off the computer, taking the ghost's advice.

The ghost is believed by many to be Hannah Hill, the daughter of the original owner Valentine Hill, who built the oldest part of the inn in 1649.

MOST HAUNTED ROOM: Hannah has been seen in the bar area and in numerous locations in the inn.

Concord's Colonial Inn is a historic hotel in Concord, Massachusetts.

CONCORD COLONIAL INN
CONCORD, MASSACHUSETTS

Imagine waking up in the middle of the night to find a Revolutionary War soldier standing at the foot of your bed. This has been the case for many visitors at the historic Concord Colonial Inn.

Built in 1716, the inn is located in Concord, Massachusetts, just down the road from the North Bridge, where the Battles of Lexington and Concord occurred. During the Revolutionary War, a portion of the inn was used to store firearms and provisions for the militia. Another section was the office of Dr. Thomas Milot. Wounded soldiers were brought to his office during the battle, and many succumbed to their injuries, lending truth to the ghostly encounters.

The inn was also home to American author Henry David Thoreau while he attended college. The building was later turned into a boarding house before being transformed into a hotel called the Thoreau House. The building was converted into an inn in 1900 and has been in operation since then, playing host to famous guests including Franklin D. Roosevelt, Shirley Temple and Bruce Springsteen.

When I had the opportunity to investigate the inn years ago, I wasn't disappointed by the activity. While we didn't see the soldier materialize in the bedroom, we did witness strange tapping sounds, shadows moving and odd smells appearing out of nowhere. While conducting an EVP (electronic voice phenomena) session in an attempt to get the resident ghosts to speak to us through our digital recorders, a lacy doily flew off the back of a chair and landed on my head, surprising me.

If you stay at the inn hoping to envelope yourself in history, you might get more than you bargained for as the history envelopes you back.

MOST HAUNTED ROOM: Room 24

The Chapman Inn is located in the heart of Bethel, Maine's historic district.

CHAPMAN INN
BETHEL, MAINE

Paranormal activity is so frequent at the Chapman Inn, the owner once brought in a paranormal investigator to dig deeper into the haunting. What he found wasn't surprising. Several ghosts were in residence, including the soul of Abigail Chapman, the invalid daughter of William Rogers Chapman, the man who originally built the house.

Abigail's life couldn't have been pleasant. Being born with an infliction, she had a live-in nanny to care for her. Since she was unable to leave the house, the nanny became her only friend. When she died at the age of sixteen, some say her soul never left the house. The investigator concluded that the other resident ghost was her companion, who didn't want to leave her young charge behind.

Staff and guests often experience cold drafts in otherwise warm rooms, unexplained footsteps in vacant areas and lights that go on and off of their own accord. Guests have been startled by whispered voices uttered breathlessly close to their ears.

One guest, in particular, had a frightening encounter. She came into her room and was surprised to find a woman wearing a white nightgown. "You're in the wrong room," she told the woman, thinking she was another guest who had somehow mistakenly ended up in her room. The woman in the nightgown just stared at her blankly before putting a finger to her lips and said, "shhhh." She then turned and walked into a wall, vanishing into thin air.

Perhaps one of the more startling hauntings is the mysterious appearance of a black cat. He is so real and solid; people often mistake him for a living cat as he darts out of the room. Most people don't realize they've seen a ghost until they report it to the staff.

Accredited as the only "certified haunted" inn in western Maine, the inn is proud of its haunted history and offers a "Come Meet the Spirits" page on its website.
MOST HAUNTED ROOMS: Rooms 7 and 9

If you decide to check out these haunted inns, be prepared for anything. If you're lucky, you might catch a few hours of sleep, but don't count on it. The dead are always eager for new nighttime playmates.

Joni Mayhan is a paranormal investigator and the author of sixteen paranormal books. To learn more about her, visit her website JoniMayhan.com.

CONCLUSION

As the author of eight historical-based ghost books, I hear all sorts of stories about alleged hauntings throughout New England. One of my readers, Michael Marciello, reached out to me about the haunting of his childhood home in Malden, Massachusetts. As a kid, he called the off-limits haunted bedroom "the bad room."

I got chills as he recounted tales of his father being pinned to the bed by an unseen force. He mentioned hearing sounds—which he later described as evil and potentially demonic—echoing from a room that was unoccupied ... at least by the living.

His mother ended up putting a lock on the bedroom's door so he and his siblings would stay away from the paranormally active first-floor room. "It was always so cold," he said, recalling the inexplicable temperature fluctuations in the bad room. "We thought it was an animal," he said, claiming that he would smell sulphur, which is an indication of an evil entity.

When I posted Marciello's account on social media, sociologist Michelle Willems talked about her version of a childhood bad room. "There was a room in my grandparents' house that was the 'wicked room.' It was my father's old bedroom, and I don't see how he ever managed to sleep there," Willems explained. "It was always about fifteen degrees colder than any other room in the house. I had a hard time even staying in the room by myself."

Barbara Tolstrup, a lifelong resident of Malden and active member of the city's historical society, interviewed me for her monthly show *Malden Square* on Malden Access TV. Like most typical New Englanders, she was initially skeptical when we talked about the paranormal. However, she opened up when I asked her if she had ever experienced a haunting in her home, which has been passed down through several generations.

"I myself have been known to be sitting in the den and then see something at the corner of my eye through the double doors in the living room," Tolstrup recalled. "I look again, and there's nothing there. This happens frequently."

Tolstrup told me that visitors have had similar ghostly encounters. She suspects it's her grandfather or great-grandfather keeping an eye on the family's decades-old home. "It probably is a family member because the house has been in our family for a hundred years."

As a paranormal researcher, I generally stay away from residential hauntings. Why? Because the phenomenon hits a little too close to home for me. I had my own experience with a "bad room," and it was my bedroom and office in a creepy old Victorian home on Hall Avenue in the Boston area.

At many haunted locations scattered throughout New England, a "cellar dweller" hides in the basement. *Photo by Frank C. Grace.*

While writing my first book, *Ghosts of Boston: Haunts of the Hub* in 2012, my sensitivity to what could be the spirit realm kicked into high gear. In fact, my old home in Somerville's Davis Square apparently had a playful older female poltergeist with an affinity for scissors. One night, I invited a friend over who claimed to have some sort of psychic ability. He said that she was a seamstress and mentioned, without hesitation, the various things she did in the house to make her presence known.

While writing the book, an unseen force opened doors that were firmly shut. Lights mysteriously turned on and off without provocation. According to my former roommate, scissors have disappeared and then reappeared over the years in the three-floor Gothic-decorated home. One night while I was writing into the wee hours on the Boston Harbor Islands' Lady in Black myth, I noticed a gray-haired female figure wearing an old-school white nightgown and fuzzy slippers dart across the first floor. I ran downstairs and noticed that the closet door had been mysteriously opened and the lights turned on while I was upstairs hacking away at my computer. My roommate was out of town. No one else was there.

The poltergeist activity on Hall Avenue turned inexplicably dark around Halloween of 2012.

After writing my second book, *Ghosts of Cambridge*, I fled my room with a "boo!" in Somerville's Davis Square. It was May 2013. Since the initial encounter, the ghostly incidents had escalated.

When I was preparing for the launch party for my first book at Boston's Old South Meeting House, the scissors sitting on the front-room table mysteriously started to spin, and one night, during an interview with Paranormal State's Ryan Buell's *Paranormal Insider Radio*, I heard a loud knock on my bedroom door. I quickly opened it, but no one was there. Oddly, the phantom knocking continued throughout the phone interview. I wasn't afraid.

Months after I submitted the manuscript for *Ghosts of Boston*, a construction crew was hired to paint the exterior of the house. Apparently, the spirit I called "Scissor Sister" didn't like the ruckus outside. What was supposed to be a month-long project turned into more than a year. The first crew of painters claimed that paint brushes would disappear and ladders would fall. One guy, tormented by a series of inexplicable incidents, asked me if the place was haunted. I nodded, and I never saw him again. After a series of freaked-out painters, scaffolding from the top floor fell on my roommate's car.

The gig was up. I decided to move.

Master psychic Denise Fix picked up on the spirit of the seamstress during our second interview. "She's not trying to scare you. She wants your attention," Fix said, sitting at a table that, oddly, was a repurposed Singer sewing machine. "She sewed for many people and felt quite tortured a lot of the time. She was celebrated by you, and she thanks you for that. She was released from whatever bound her there," Fix continued. "And it wasn't a good thing to be bound there."

Two weeks later, I moved out. My last night in the house was memorable. My roommate's exotic parrot escaped from its cage and perched on the oven's open flame. The bird was quickly engulfed in flames but didn't catch fire. The bird was unharmed. While carrying boxes down the stairs, I slipped. I felt something hold me back as I watched the box fall down the stairs. Glass shattered. It could have been me. I fled the haunted house on Hall Avenue and haven't looked back ... until now.

Peter Muise, a friend and fellow History Press author, posted about a bizarre cryptid encounter from the 1980s on his blog *New England Folklore*.

"A young woman named Karen bought a Victorian-era house outside of Somerville's Davis Square in 1983. She liked living there, but there were a few things that seemed a little odd. The basement often flooded, which was annoying, but Karen suspected that something else was going on," Muise wrote.

"She often felt uncomfortable near the back wall of her house, particularly on the second and third floors. She kept her spare clothing up on the third floor but got such weird vibes that she did not go up there at night. She had tried sleeping in the back bedroom on the second floor, but did so only briefly because she felt uncomfortable there as well. She felt that there was something in the room with her at night," he continued.

Karen was featured in *The Ghostly Register* by Arthur Myers. "I had a feeling of a presence at night, of its being almost like an an animal, as though it had claws or wanted to bite me," she recalled.

According to *The Ghostly Register*, Karen and her roommate reached out to a Cambridge psychic who said the poltergeist-like activity wasn't a ghost ... but a troll.

"The troll was apparently connected with an underground spring that ran under the house and that caused the basement flooding," Muise explained. "When the house was built on top of the spring, the troll became trapped and would send its energy up along the back wall of the house. Karen had always felt its presence in the house, but the troll increased its activity once the roommate moved in and started to sleep near that wall."

The troll supposedly revealed himself during the ritual and begged Karen to let him stay. She asked the cryptid to leave, and the troll haunting and basement flooding mysteriously stopped.

However, did the cryptid have any ties to my paranormal encounter in 2012? After reading Muise's post, it turns out the troll incident was literally across the street from my old home on Hall Avenue.

"I am so curious where in the Davis Square area this happened. I lived in a Victorian near Davis Square and had what we believed to be a poltergeist who had an affinity for scissors ... maybe she was a troll?" I joked online. However, Muise's response made my jaw drop.

"According to Myers, the troll house was 35 Hall Ave. It's weird there is so much strange phenomena on one street," he responded. I gasped. My old home on Hall Avenue was a stone's throw from the troll incident in the 1980s.

Muise suggested that maybe the troll just moved across the street. Or perhaps Karen was experiencing poltergeist activity and somehow mistook it for a mythical monster. For the record, there was a movie called *Troll* that came out around the time of this alleged cryptid encounter.

Did whatever Karen and her roommate experience in the 1980s somehow set up shop across the street? In hindsight, I believe it did.

SOURCES

Updated excerpts from my first seven books, including *Ghosts of Boston: Haunts of the Hub, Ghosts of Salem: Haunts of the Witch City and 13 Most Haunted in Massachusetts* were featured in *13 Most Haunted Hotels & Inns of New England*. The material in this book is drawn from published sources, including issues of *Boston Spirit, The Independent, Boston Globe, Boston Herald, The Ghostly Register, Metrowest Daily, The New York Times, Patriot Ledger* and *SouthCoast Today* and television programs such as *TLC's Kindred Spirits, Destination America's Haunted Towns, Travel Channel's Ghost Adventures* and *Syfy's Ghost Hunters*. Several books on New England's paranormal history were used and cited throughout the text. Other New England–based websites and periodicals such as my various newspaper and magazine articles on the paranormal, Joni Mayhan's work for *Ghost Diaries* and Peter Muise's blog *New England Folklore* served as primary sources. I also conducted firsthand interviews, and some of the material is drawn from my own research. The Boston-based ghost tour, *Boston Haunts*, was also a major source of information and generated original content. My tours in Salem, Cambridge, Boston Harbor and Provincetown also served as inspiration for the book. It should be noted that ghost stories are subjective, and I have made a concerted effort to stick to the historical facts, even if it resulted in debunking an alleged encounter with the paranormal.

Baltrusis, Sam. *Ghosts of Boston: Haunts of the Hub*. Charleston, SC: The History Press, 2012.

Baltrusis, Sam. *Ghosts of Cambridge: Haunts of Harvard Square and Beyond*. Charleston, SC: The History Press, 2013.

Baltrusis, Sam. *Ghosts of Salem: Haunts of the Witch City*. Charleston, SC: The History Press, 2014.

Brennan, John T. *Ghosts of Newport: Spirits, Scoundrels, Legends and Lore*. Charleston, SC: The History Press, 2007.

D'Agostino, Thomas. *A Guide to Haunted New England*. Charleston, SC: The History Press, 2009.

Forest, Christopher. *North Shore Spirits of Massachusetts*. Atglen, PA: Schiffer Publishing, 2003.

Gellerman, Bruce and Sherman, Erik. *Massachusetts Curiosities*. Guilford, CT: The Globe Pequot Press, 2005.

Hall, Thomas. *Shipwrecks of Massachusetts Bay*. Charleston, SC: The History Press, 2012.

Hauk, Dennis William. *Haunted Places: The National Directory.* New York: Penguin Group, 1996.

Jasper, Mark. *Haunted Cape Cod & The Islands.* Yarmouthport, MA: On Cape Publications, 2002.

Jasper, Mark. *Haunted Inns of New England.* Yarmouthport, MA: On Cape Publications, 2000.

Mayhan, Joni. *Dark and Scary Things.* Gardner, MA: Joni Mayhan, 2015.

Muise, Peter. *Legends and Lore of the North Shore.* Charleston, SC: The History Press, 2014.

Nadler, Holly Mascott. *Ghosts of Boston Town: Three Centuries of True Hauntings.* Camden, ME: Down East Books, 2002.

Norman, Michael and Scott, Beth. *Historic Haunted America.* New York, NY: Tor Books, 1995.

Ogden, Tom. *The Complete Idiot's Guide to Ghosts & Hauntings.* Indianapolis, IN: Alpha Books, 2004.

Raven, Rory. *Haunted Providence.* Charleston, SC: The History Press, 2008.

Revai, Cheri. Haunted Massachusetts: Ghosts and Strange Phenomena of the Bay State. Mechanicsburg, PA: Stackpole Books, 2005.

Zwicker, Roxie. Haunted York County: Mystery and Lore from Maine's Oldest Towns. Charleston, SC: The History Press, 2010.

Sam Baltrusis, author of *13 Most Haunted Hotels & Inns of New England*, was featured on Destination America and the Travel Channel where he recounted his ghostly experiences in Salem, Massachusetts. *Photo by Gina Bengston.*

ABOUT THE AUTHOR

Sam Baltrusis, author of *Ghosts of Boston* and *Ghosts of Salem*, has penned eight historical-based ghost books. He has been featured on several national TV shows, including Destination America's *Haunted Towns* and the Travel Channel episode on Salem, and has served as Boston's paranormal expert on the Biography Channel's *Haunted Encounters*. Baltrusis moonlights as a tour guide and launched the successful ghost tours, Boston Haunts and the Wicked Salem Tour. He had several books come out in 2016, including *13 Most Haunted Crime Scenes*, *Haunted Boston Harbor* and *Paranormal Provincetown*. Baltrusis is also a sought-after lecturer who speaks at dozens of paranormal-related events scattered throughout New England, including an author discussion at the Massachusetts State House. In the past, he has worked for VH1, MTV.com, *Newsweek* and ABC Radio and as a regional stringer for the *New York Times*. Visit 13MostHaunted.com for more information.